Blessing

For Christine, Natalie and Ruth,
and for Rachel and Sally

FAITH GOING DEEPER

Blessing

Andrew Davison

CANTERBURY
PRESS
Norwich

© Andrew Davison 2014

First published in 2014 by the Canterbury Press Norwich
Editorial office
3rd Floor, Invicta House,
108–114 Golden Lane,
London EC1Y 0TG

Canterbury Press is an imprint of Hymns Ancient & Modern Ltd
(a registered charity)
13A Hellesdon Park Road, Norwich,
Norfolk NR6 5DR, UK

www.canterburypress.co.uk

British Library Cataloguing in Publication data

A catalogue record for this book is available
from the British Library

978 1 84825 642 2

Typeset by Manila Typesetting
Printed and bound in Great Britain by
CPI Group (UK) Ltd, Croydon, CR0 4YY

Contents

PART I

Blessing in Christian Theology

1

Creation: Recognition, Thanksgiving and Praise

Christ's last act before his Ascension was to bless his disciples:

> he led them out as far as Bethany, and, lifting up his hands, he blessed them. While he was blessing them, he withdrew from them and was carried up into heaven. And they worshipped him, and returned to Jerusalem with great joy; and they were continually in the temple blessing God. (Luke 24.50–53)[1]

This is the image of Christ fixed in our minds by his departure: Christ blessing. That theme is then immediately taken up, in this passage, now among the disciples. For their part, they devoted themselves to praise in the temple or, as Luke calls it, to 'blessing God'.

Here, at this crucial juncture in the Gospel story, we are presented with two of the most significant meanings of blessing: as a benediction bestowed and as praise given. Blessing is central at this turning point in the story of Christ, which underlines the significance of blessing as a

---

1 Unless otherwise stated, translations of the Bible are taken from the New Revised Standard Version, Anglicized Edition.

theological topic – and yet, as a subject, blessing has not received a great deal of theological discussion. As one scholar has recently put it, blessing has 'received relatively little attention from theologians and liturgists before the twentieth century'.[2] The priest and poet George Herbert (1593–1633) made a similar point when he remarked that his fellow priests were apt to treat blessing as 'empty and superfluous'. But, he went on:

> that which the Apostles used so diligently in their writings, nay, which our Saviour himself used (Mark 10.16), cannot be vain and superfluous . . . Besides, the Priests of the Old Testament were commanded to bless the people, and the form thereof is prescribed (Num. 6.22–27). Now as the Apostle argues in another case, if the ministration of condemnation did bless, how shall not the ministration of the Spirit exceed in blessing?[3]

There is mismatch between the prominence of blessing in the Scriptures and the attention it has received in theology. That would be enough to invite a study such as this, but there are other reasons, not least as part of an attempt to explore the range of registers in which the ministry and mission of the Church can be carried out. Personally, as one who particularly respects the traditions

---

2 Uwe Michael Lang, 'Theologies of Blessing: Origins and Characteristics of *De benedictionibus* (1984)', *Antiphon* 15.1 (2011), pp. 27–46, p. 43. Marcus Donovan judged, in 1925, that we retain only 'a few relics of the principle, e.g. in saying grace over our meals, but for the most part blessing has dropped out of our practice, and is inadequately replaced in a few instances by superstitious ceremonies of dedication (e.g. of a battleship) or formal opening of a civic of municipal building' – *Sacramentals* (London: Society of SS. Peter & Paul, 1925), p. 30.

3 George Herbert, *The Country Parson*, Ch. 36, spelling and punctuation modernized.

of the Dominican Order, I am drawn by the threefold pattern set out in one of their mottos: *Laudare, Benedicere, Praedicare* ('To praise, to bless, to preach'). We have a sense of what it means to have a vocation to praise, and perhaps what it might mean to have a vocation to preach, but what – we might ask – does it mean to be called to bless?

As we set out to explore the meaning of blessing, we should recognize that it is a broad category. We have already seen the word function in two senses at the end of Luke: related senses, assuredly, but certainly not identical. These are as a benediction bestowed and as praise offered. Part 1 of this book will consider some of these dimensions. A good place to start is with speech. To bless is to speak. That is obvious enough, since blessing is always a matter of communication, one way or another: words are spoken; some communicative gesture is often made. Moreover, often something *from God* is being communicated to whatever or whomever is being blessed.

The significance of speech is borne out by the etymology of a related word, namely 'benediction'. Its English root is in the Latin *benedicere*, which is grounded in the idea of 'speaking well' of something: from *bene*, meaning good (as in benefit), and *dicere* meaning to speak (as in diction).[4] In this opening chapter of the book we will explore just this, and consider what it means for blessing to be about 'speaking well' – first of creation and then of God.

---

4 Latin is the vehicle for the Western Christian tradition but the Greek word for blessing carries exactly the same sense: *eulogein* – again, 'to speak well'. This is the Greek word used to translate the Hebrew word for 'to bless' (*barak*) in the standard Greek translation of the Old Testament, the Septuagint, which is the translation known by the New Testament authors.

Ask someone on the street what blessings mean or achieve, and the most common response is likely to be that they *make* something holy, 'good' or special. That sense is certainly important but we will begin somewhere else, with the doctrine of creation and the conviction that a blessing is about *recognition* as well as *conferral*. Whatever else we are doing when we bless someone, something or somewhere, we recognize that all God has made is already good, already possesses a certain holiness, precisely since it comes to us from God's hands.

A blessing recognizes the goodness of God's creation. This links blessing to a central task of Christian discipleship, namely learning to see the world from a Christian perspective. Much of what we call Christian ethics is to be found in that discipline and goal. The Christian moral life is not primarily a set of rules to be followed but a way of perceiving, from which the right action naturally follows. Whatever else it involves, such a perception of the world, in a Christian way, includes beholding it with a sense of wonder and apprehending it in such a way that we recognize it as a gift. Those dispositions, in turn, elicit praise from us, and thanksgiving.

The practice of blessing things is first of all about opening our eyes, so that praise and thanksgiving arise often and spontaneously. Part of the reason that we bless is to develop the habit of seeing the world in a way that elicits responses of praise and wonder. As a recognition, as well as conferral, blessing is an act of *reception* – of reception with a thankful spirit. We are in territory here discussed in 1 Timothy, where we read the precept that 'everything created by God is good, and nothing is to be rejected, provided it is received with thanksgiving' (1 Tim. 4.4). One of the earliest Christian liturgical texts to have survived, the *Apostolic Tradition* (probably from the second to fourth century), echoes this injunction: 'for everything we receive we should give thanks to God the Holy One, receiving it in this way for his glory'.[5] If blessing is about speech, then learning from the Christian tradition about blessing must also discipline the way we speak about creation. Blessing is a way to 'speak well' of creation, to recognize it as God's work and as God's gift to us.

However, before we can speak, God has already spoken. Creation *itself* is already God's primordial 'speaking well'. Through speech – as the metaphor at the beginning of Genesis has it – God brought creation into being. God created through a word, which theologians have described as his Word, with a capital letter, or his Son (John 1). That Word brought everything into being and invested it with character, meaning and significance. That, after all, is what speech is all about: character, meaning and significance.

In the Genesis story, at the end of each 'day' God looked at the world and 'saw that it is good'. After God's creative 'speaking well', he 'recognized' that what he had made is good. In blessing we follow in God's footsteps: we 'see that it is good'. In the Genesis narrative, God himself pronounces blessing upon creation: first upon sea creatures and birds (Gen. 1.22) and then on human beings (Gen. 1.28).[6]

If blessing is about a way of seeing, then it aligns with other Christian practices, of which a particularly important

---

5 *Apostolic Tradition*, 32. Quoted in Mark Drew, 'Introduction', in Sean Finnegan (ed.), *Consecrations, Blessings and Prayers* (London: Canterbury Press, 2005), p. x.

6 God does not, on the sixth day, seem to bless the other creatures created on that day – the other animals. It is not clear why this is so. Perhaps, because human beings are blessed to have dominion over the other creatures, it would be inappropriate for them to be blessed alongside human beings.

example is contemplative prayer. As David Bentley Hart has put it, such prayer is 'an extremely simple thing':

> It often consists in little more than cultivating certain habits of thought, certain ways of seeing reality, certain acts of openness to a grace that one cannot presume but that has already been granted, in some very substantial measure, in the mere givenness of existence.[7]

Blessing occupies a place in the life of the Church as just such a 'habit of thought', a way 'of seeing reality', an act by which we are open 'to a grace that one cannot presume but that has already been granted . . . in the mere givenness of existence'.

We see this connection, between blessing and recognition, in the account of Jesus being presented in the temple in Jerusalem 40 days after his birth (Luke 2.22–38). The purpose of the visit was a rather solemn kind of blessing: it is called a 'presentation' and it is clearly a form of consecration. Its purpose was to 'designate' every firstborn male 'as holy to the Lord' (Luke 2.23). Simeon, the priest, took the Christ child up into his arms and, after he had proclaimed the song we call the *Nunc Dimittis*, he 'blessed them' – child and parents. Blessing is linked here to recognition, since that canticle is precisely a song of recognition:[8]

> Master, now you are dismissing your servant in peace, according to your word;
> for my eyes have seen your salvation,
> which you have prepared in the presence of all peoples,

---

7 David Bentley Hart, *The Experience of God: Being, Consciousness, Bliss* (New Haven, CT: Yale University Press, 2013), pp. 321–2.

8 The link is made by Martyn Percy in *Thirty-Nine New Articles* (London: Canterbury Press, 2013), p. 83.

a light for revelation to the Gentiles
and for glory to your people Israel. (Luke 2.29–32)

For another sign of this link between blessing and the recognition of goodness, we might consider their negation. Down church history, various heretics simply could not have made much sense of our practice of blessing, and precisely because of its association with 'speaking well' of creation. Gnosticism, in its various guises, saw the material world as the work of an evil god. For Gnostics, therefore, material things are basically evil, at least in as much as they are material. They would not bless material things – or human beings in their bodyliness or places in their physicality – whereas orthodox Christians would. A Christian would bless what is good but refuse to bless something orientated towards evil; the Gnostic would not bless anything material at all, because they saw materiality as sinful to its core.

In Part 2 of this book we will consider some of the ways blessing could feature more centrally in the life of the Church, of individual Christians and of households. A good place to start is with blessing as thankful recognition, not least in the most common of 'blessings': what we call grace or the blessing of a meal. This theme also suggests that any services or occasions for blessing should contain some explicit mention that God is creator and some explicit recognition that what we bless has come from him.

Blessing and Praise

As we have seen, to bless is to speak, and an important part of that is to acknowledge, by word and gesture, that the thing, person or situation that we bless is a gift from

God. Blessing turns out to be an excellent confession of Christian belief in the doctrine of creation. From speaking well of the creation in this way, we are only a short step from speaking well of the creator. Just such a 'speaking well' of God is what lies behind the injunction, found throughout the Bible, that we should 'bless the Lord'. On the face of it, this is a strange form of words. If we see blessing, in some restricted way, as only an act by which something is made good or made holy, then 'blessing God' hardly makes sense. God is already all-holy and all-good. Moreover, if blessing is simply an act by which God makes things good and holy, then the idea of us blessing God is even stranger. If, however, we see that blessing is also a recognition, then 'blessing God' becomes more intelligible. It recognizes God's goodness or holiness, rather than establishing it. Or, if we want to explore that 'establishing' avenue all the same, then 'blessing God' will not be about establishing God's holiness *in itself*; it will be about establishing the truth of God's goodness and holiness within the culture in which we live. We do not make God holy but we can help our world to make a better attempt at recognizing God's holiness and keeping it in mind. For a parallel we might consider the words of the Blessed Virgin Mary: 'My soul doth magnify the Lord' (Luke 1.46, AV). Mary was not *making* God greater by her praise; she was proclaiming his greatness. She was not enlarging God's grandeur in itself; she was enlarging the honour ascribed to him within the world. Christians have used her words to carry on doing just that ever since.

Blessing, then, takes in speaking well of God as well as speaking well of his creation. That, in turn, has suggested a second element that should also be present in every act of blessing, namely some element of praise. We see that in words that open a common form of prayer of blessing:

'Blessed art thou, Lord God of all creation.' Just as a blessing properly includes recognition of God as creator, it should also ascribe praise to God and recognize his holiness.

In the liturgy of the Church we find all of creation called upon to 'bless the Lord' by way of praise. This is found particularly in the canticle known as the *Benedicite* (or the *Song of the Three Children*), which is taken from the Prayer of Azariah (vv. 35–66), a book that is in the Apocrypha for some Christians and in the Old Testament for others. In this great song of praise, all the 'works of the Lord' are to 'bless the Lord': 'Sun and Moon . . . Showers and Dew . . . Beasts and Cattle . . . Children of Men'.[9] We can say that each is called to praise God through its own distinctive excellence, according to its own kind: the sun in its brightness, the moon in its lustre, showers and dew in their wetness, and so on. Each praises God, we can say, by achieving its distinctive vocation, and it is to this topic that we now turn.

9 Prayer Book translation.

2

Vocation: Abundance and Consecration

Blessing is linked to speech. We have already seen this twice over: first, blessing involves recognition of the goodness of what God has *called* into existence; we called that God's primordial 'speaking well' of things. Then blessing is also praise: our 'speaking well' of God as creator of all. That recognition might be ours, and that praise might be ours, but blessing is God's work before it is ours. Blessing, fundamentally, comes *from* God, and any individual blessing is part of the unfolding story of his blessing. As Gordon Lathrop puts it, 'A thing or person is "blessed" by gathering that thing or person verbally into the story of God.'[1]

Right from the first book of the Bible we are presented with the story of God blessing his people. God addresses the human couple, for instance, and invokes blessing upon them (Gen. 1.28). He blesses Abraham (Gen. 15.5; 22.17–18), again invoking progeny (with one particular successor, Jesus Christ, seen by the Church fulfilling and perfecting this blessing), and he blesses Jacob, and on direct account of that he receives the new name of 'Israel' (Gen. 26.3–4, 12–13).

---

1 Gordon Lathrop, *Holy Ground: A Liturgical Cosmology* (Minneapolis, MN: Fortress Press, 2003), p. 86.

These examples demonstrate that the biblical vision of blessing is closely connected with another form of speaking, namely with vocation. Like the Latinate word 'benediction', our word 'vocation' comes from a root concerned with speech: from calling (*vocare*). 'Calling' and 'vocation' mean the same in English; to receive a vocation is to be called. With the blessing upon Adam and Eve the vocation is to be fruitful and fill the earth; with the blessing on Abraham the calling is to follow God in faith and to become, thereby, the father of his chosen people. That way, God's blessing is to come to the whole earth. Abraham's blessing, and this vocation, are taken up by Jacob, most specifically in the scene at the River Jabbok, where he refuses to let go of the angel, who represents God, until he has been blessed (Gen. 32.22–32).

Applying this to the life of the Church, this link between vocation and blessing runs both ways: when we discern a vocation, we bless it, and when we bless something, we impart, invoke or recognize some sense of vocation – some sort of duty or new trajectory into the future. We bless vocations at a variety of moments in the life of the Church and in the lives of individual Christians, either when a vocation is publically acknowledged or when some specific authority or recognition is conferred, in line with a vocation that has been discerned. The sacrament of marriage is one example, when a vocation is recognized and affirmed by the Church, as is confirmation or ordination, where a vocation is similarly recognized and affirmed, and when the Church invests a certain authority in an individual. In the later twentieth century new prominence was given, across the Church, to services of commissioning for lay ministry.

There is no coincidence to the observation that each of the liturgical recognitions of vocation just mentioned take the form of a blessing: a marriage typically has a blessing at its heart, as does a commissioning service, and while we are perhaps not as used to thinking about ordination or confirmation as blessings, they clearly are so.

With these examples we see that God's blessing is not simply something general but is also specific. God does indeed bless the world as a whole in its creation but God also blesses specifically. The primary example of this in the Bible is the blessing of the people of Israel, and then of Christ and of the Church, as inheritors of the blessing of Israel. That has repercussions for blessings in the Church. There too the blessing of the whole is worked out in terms of the blessing of the specific.

Blessing, then, is an appropriate way to mark and respond to a vocation. In a parallel fashion a blessing of any kind brings a calling along with it: a vocation and a certain set of responsibilities. This points us to the element of blessing that is called consecration: something – or someone or somewhere – that has been consecrated has been dedicated to a certain task or role. In each of the examples just given – marriage, blessing of a lay ministry, ordination and confirmation – the Church recognizes, certainly, but she also bestows and begins. There is an inception and a redirection; lives have a new trajectory. A building that is blessed as a place of worship can be said to receive a vocation. Even linen blessed for use on an altar has received a new 'calling'. That may sound a little wayward or exaggerated, but such a statement actually throws considerable light on what vocation means and therefore on what blessing means. Blessing altar linen changes what this particular piece of cloth is *for*. This sort of blessing marks and effects a change of use. That could hardly bear more directly on the territory of vocation: to discern your vocation is to discern what you are for, what your life is for. A blessing associated with that vocation serves to confirm this.

The conjunction of blessing and vocation helps us to see that blessings are not, therefore, to be conferred lightly. We would not want, lightly, to set anyone on a particular trajectory in life, since every vocation has its responsibilities and one vocation can be incompatible with another, although equally valuable. This observation bears most obviously on marriage. As the Church of England's Prayer Book has it, marriage is not to be entered into 'unadvisedly, lightly, or wantonly . . . but reverently, discreetly, advisedly, soberly, and in the fear of God'. Ordination is another example. That same Prayer Book provides a prayer (or 'collect') for the days running up to an ordination, which asks God to guide the bishops so that 'they may lay hands suddenly [i.e. hastily] on no man, but faithfully and wisely make choice of fit persons to serve in the sacred Ministry of thy Church'.[2] We do not bless lightly.

Abundance

Given the link between blessing and vocation, we should note that the vocation that God holds out for his people is one of blessing and of life, as seen for instance, in Deuteronomy 30, at the beginning of Genesis or in that 'life in all its fullness' that Christ came to bring (John 10.10). On the fifth day God blessed the birds and the creatures of the sea: 'God blessed them, saying, "Be fruitful and multiply and fill the waters in the seas, and let birds multiply on the earth"' (Gen. 1.22). The vision here is quite

---

2 The first prayer 'In the Ember Weeks', from the 'Prayers and Thanksgivings', alluding to 1 Timothy 5.22. Happily, are now include women alongside the men.

explicitly one of abundance or, we might say, of *fullness*: the vocation of creatures is to 'be fruitful and multiply' so as to *fill out* the whole sphere of creation proper to them. Shortly after, on the sixth day, we come across the first and original blessing pronounced upon the human race. Once again it is concerned with fruitfulness and the expansion of one's domain – or perhaps we should say of expansions *into* one's domain:

> God blessed them, and God said to them, 'Be fruitful and multiply, and fill the earth and subdue it; and have dominion over the fish of the sea and over the birds of the air and over every living thing that moves upon the earth.' (Gen. 1.28)

Fruitfulness is part of what it means for a creature to live, to be alive. That corresponds to a scientific sense of the distinctive properties of living things: among them is the observation that living things reproduce. This creativity is one of the ways every living thing participates, in some way, in the image of God, even if that image is found most perfectly in human beings (and angels):[3] God has created and multiplied them, and he allows them to participate in his creativity by themselves reproducing.[4]

Just such a connection to fruitfulness and progeny is also seen in the blessing upon Abraham and upon Jacob, as we have just seen. Abraham's blessing is that he will be the

---

3 Aquinas distinguished between the 'image' in human beings – and angels – and a 'trace' in other creatures. The Latin is *vestigium*, meaning footprint. I discuss this in my book *Participation* (Eugene, OR: Wipf & Stock, 2015).

4 Bill T. Arnold makes the point in his commentary: *Genesis* (Cambridge: Cambridge University Press, 2009), p. 43.

father of many nations and that, through him, blessing will come to all the nations of the earth:

> I will indeed bless you, and I will make your offspring as numerous as the stars of heaven and as the sand that is on the seashore. And your offspring shall possess the gate of their enemies, and by your offspring shall all the nations of the earth gain blessing for themselves, because you have obeyed my voice. (Gen. 22.17–18)[5]

This blessing is repeated, in much the same words, to his son Isaac (Gen. 26.3–4), after which we read that 'The LORD blessed him, and the man became rich; he prospered more and more until he became very wealthy' (Gen. 26.12–13). Later, Jacob entered into this blessing, although by stealth, tricking it from his brother Esau (Gen. 27). Having snatched it from Esau, he later wrests its confirmation (literally – he wrestles for it) from an angelic representative of God (Gen. 32.22–32).

In these accounts, blessing is strongly bound up with earthly success and prosperity. Most of all it is cast in terms of the fruitfulness of the womb: many offspring (as in each of these cases) and many cattle and servants (with the Abrahamic blessing and its reiterations).[6] Alongside these themes belong the abundance of the earth in bringing forth both crops and an abundance of raw materials for building and commerce. We find these forms of abundance grouped together throughout the Old Testament, for instance in some of the psalms.[7]

These psalms are particularly those associated with the 'wisdom' tradition, and the link between God's favour and blessing is explored throughout this literature, for instance

---

5 Echoing Genesis 15.5.
6 For example in Genesis 26.14.
7 Examples include Psalms 1, 5, 84 and 144.

in Proverbs. That said, the problems with this association are also explored there. While it is difficult to date these books exactly, or their component parts, we can reasonably suggest that the more uncomplicated association between material blessing and God's favour – or with doing right – belongs to an earlier stratum, while later on the question of the suffering of the righteous, and the prosperity of the unrighteous, becomes more of a matter for consideration. Psalm 37 is a notable example, and we find a certain ambivalence there. On the one hand it makes a link between righteousness and material blessing: 'Trust in the LORD, and do good; so you will live in the land, and enjoy security' (v. 3), and even more emphatically, 'I have been young, and now am old, yet I have not seen the righteous forsaken or their children begging bread' (v. 25). On the other hand, it sees that this association is not always played out historically, at least not in the short term: sometimes the wicked have an 'abundance' and the righteous have 'little' (v. 16).[8] All the same, the overall mood is one of confidence that the righteous will flourish, eventually, and the wicked suffer: 'the arms of the wicked shall be broken, but the LORD upholds the righteous' (v. 17).

The problem of a disparity between blessing and prosperity is placed in an even more acute context in the book of Job and in Ecclesiastes. Consider this passage from Job:

Why do the wicked live on,
    reach old age, and grow mighty in power?
Their children are established in their presence,
    and their offspring before their eyes.

---

8 We might also consider the rather striking comment, or admission even, that 'Many are the afflictions of the righteous, but the LORD rescues them from them all' (Ps. 34.19).

Their houses are safe from fear,
   and no rod of God is upon them.
Their bull breeds without fail;
   their cow calves and never miscarries.
They send out their little ones like a flock,
   and their children dance around . . .
What is the Almighty, that we should serve him?
   And what profit do we get if we pray to him?
   (Job 21.7–11, 15).

This question of prosperity is of the first importance for any contemporary consideration of blessing, not least because of the global significance of the 'prosperity gospel' movement. We will return to that below, in Chapter 3.

Blessing and Beseeching

Our tone so far has been one of celebration and affirmation. That cannot be the whole picture, however. Part of why we bless is the recognition that nothing is quite as it should be. Blessing might take the doctrine of creation seriously but it also considers the doctrine of the Fall. A blessing contains an inescapable element of restoration – a sense of elevation or of rescuing from profanity. We will not let profanity have the last word but we do not ignore it.

Blessings note that all is not entirely well with the world. That also finds expression in our recognition that there are things and situations that we should not bless and perhaps cannot bless. Many Christians would find a certain obscenity in the sight of a priest blessing a bomb or missile. Many – if not all – churches have some teaching about which sorts of relationships ought to receive the Church's blessing and which not. We might not all agree on the list but we would probably agree that there *are* certain things and situations that should not be blessed, whatever they might be. We could not appropriately bless the opening of a shop in a low-income area dedicated to lending money at extortionate rates of interest, for example.

Even in this solemn recognition of what we should not bless we should find hope. The observation that we should not bless certain things confirms that blessing is intrinsically orientated to the recognition of goodness. We have a sense of what can not be blessed *because* blessing is about goodness. Similarly the observation that all is not right with the world should serve to confirm the yet more fundamental conviction, upon which it must rest, that the world *was* created to be good. Were that not so, we would not apprehend the fact that it is not always good as such a *mistake*.

In blessing there is the aspect centred on celebration, through a recognition of creation as God's good gift, and there is another, centred on purification or the invocation of God's aid, which acknowledges that all is not right with the world or ourselves. On this front the Lutheran scholar Gordon Lathrop has provided a helpful analysis. He takes names for these two aspects of blessing from two principal features of typical eucharistic rites – perhaps *the* two principal aspects: on the one hand *remembering* and on the other *calling down*. To give them their Greek names, we have *anamnesis* and *epiclesis*.[9] These line up with what Lathrop calls the elements to blessing of 'thanksgiving' and 'beseeching', and to Christian prayer more widely.[10] Each has its proper place: 'The thanksgiving should be honest about the goodness of the earth and its structures. The beseeching

---

9 Lathrop, *Holy Ground*, p. 87.
10 Lathrop, *Holy Ground*, p. 85.

should insist on remembering those who are outside such goodness, blowing a hole in any status quo.'[11]

This analysis of blessing in terms of thanksgiving, or something like it, and of a prayer for salvation, or something like it, can be found throughout the theological tradition, even if it is not always put in such crystalline eucharistic terms as we find in Lathrop.[12] For instance, Ambrose of Milan described a blessing (with reversed order here) as 'the conferral of sanctification and the rendering of thanks'.[13] The *Catechism of the Catholic Church* notes that 'Every blessing praises God and prays for his gifts'[14] and that blessings 'include both praise of God for his works and gifts, and the Church's intercession for men [*sic*] that they may be able to use God's gifts according to the spirit of the Gospel'.[15]

To make a point that will run throughout this book, blessings are right and proper on their own terms but also serve a tutelary purpose. By becoming people who bless and are blessed, and a church that blesses and is blessed, we are taught to look at the world in certain terms. Lathrop makes this point in terms of his twofold distinction: we can be shaped by the liturgy to live lives of thankfulness and beseeching without knowing how to analyse technically how the liturgy does this.[16] This way of looking at the world is not the preserve 'of the learned or the critical'.

---

11 Lathrop, *Holy Ground*, p. 87.

12 Although Mark Drew also makes use of the eucharistic distinction – 'Introduction', in Sean Finnegan (ed.), *Consecrations, Blessings and Prayers* (London: Canterbury Press, 2005), pp. vii–viii.

13 *De Benedictionibus Patriarcharum*, ch. 22. Quoted in Drew, 'Introduction', p. x.

14 *Catechism of the Catholic Church* (London: Burns & Oates, 2004; see also www.vatican.va/archive/ENG0015/_INDEX.HTM), §1671.

15 *Catechism of the Catholic Church*, §1678.

16 Lathrop, *Holy Ground*, p. 88.

Consecration

Blessing rightly belongs to the sunnier side of Christian theology but we would be remiss to deny that blessing comes with a cost. That is clear enough from the biblical examples: Abraham's blessing went along with a call to give up everything, to travel to an alien land and even to be willing to give up his son (Gen. 11; 22). Jacob, for his part, received the blessing he requested from the angel but thereafter always walked with a limp (Gen. 32.22–32).

The aspect of blessing associated with foregoing has often been called 'consecration'.[17] We have come across it already. We might think of Samson foregoing wine (Judg. 13.4–5), or that the priests and Levites went without a provision of lands (Josh. 18.7), or of that 'forsaking all other' upon which marriage is built. This connection exists but it is not about a glorification of loss or of difficulty. The point is rather to stress that blessing demands something of us – everything worthwhile does.

Evelyn Underhill explored this connection in slightly different terms, writing that consecration always follows on from *offering* (or oblation). Blessing and sacrifice are not far removed from one another. In Christian thought and in Christian liturgy, Underhill wrote, we:

> should never separate the two movements of oblation and consecration . . . One movement supposes and completes the other; as the Nativity, God self-given in the flesh, requires the free oblation of the creature – the Blessed

---

17 The roots are *com-* (here transmuted to *con*) and *sacrare* (to make holy), *com-* acting here as an intensifying suffix.

Virgin's self-offering to His hidden purpose. 'Behold the Handmaid of the Lord! Be it unto me according to Thy word!'[18]

We might go further, saying that offering is not simply a necessary preparation for consecration but part of the very idea of consecration itself. To consecrate someone – or something or somewhere – is to set her apart. We need not see this as casting a shadow over our topic but it does remind us to approach it with seriousness. We need not have heaviness of heart, in the first place because we are talking about voluntary consecrations: no one is being compelled to offer or give up. Even more to the point, the sort of giving up we are talking about, especially in the most serious sorts of blessing, is attached to the greatest sorts of gain. We need only think, once again, of marriage as an example, where a certain sort of gain – the 'goods of marriage'[19] – can only come our way because of what we are prepared to give up: 'forsaking all other, [so as to] keep thee only unto her [or him], so long as ye both shall live'. As G. K. Chesterton put it, 'Keeping to one woman is a small price for so much as seeing one woman.'[20]

Consecration, we might say, is about the association of a thing or person with God. The 'blessedness' to which we wish to introduce whatever or whoever we bless is nothing other than a participation in the perfect and eternal

---

18 Evelyn Underhill, *The Mystery of Sacrifice* (London: Longmans, Green & Co., 1938), p. 42.

19 On these, see my *Why Sacraments?* (London: SPCK/Eugene, OR: Wipf & Stock, 2013), pp. 105–11.

20 G. K. Chesterton, *Orthodoxy* (New York: Bantam, 1996), p. 55.

blessedness of God, who is supremely blessed. Similarly, holiness is a participation in God's holiness.[21]

The biblical literature particularly associates such a participation in God's holiness with being set apart. We are not saying, of course, that *God* has been set apart. The 'apartness' of God is his transcendence, his not being a thing-among-things – and this utter transcendence is what undergirds his profound closeness to all that he has made.[22] Just as any creaturely blessedness is a participation in God's blessedness, any holiness – any setting apart or any set-apartness – is a participation in God's holiness, in God's being apart from the world. Part of what we are doing in blessing and setting things apart, and setting people and places apart, is bearing witness to the holiness of God.

If every blessing should bear witness to the holiness of God in some way, the supreme blessing, which is the Eucharist, does this most of all. Confession of God's holiness plays a prominent part in most eucharistic rites. We see it, for instance, in the recitation of the *Sanctus* ('Holy, Holy, Holy, Lord God of Hosts, Heaven and Earth are full of thy glory'), often followed by words such as 'you are holy indeed, the source of all holiness'.[23] In some of the older liturgies the confession of God's holiness takes

---

21 The adjective *blessed* is one of the few English words that sometimes comes with an accent: *blessèd*. Although this older convention might occasionally help the reader to distinguish between the adjectival usage and the participle, I have opted not to use the accented form.

22 See, for instance, my *The Love of Wisdom: An Introduction to Philosophy for Theologians* (London: SCM Press, 2013), pp. 187–8, and *Participation*.

23 As, in this case, in the Church of England Eucharistic Prayer B in *Common Worship: Main Volume* (London: Church House Publishing, 2000), p. 189.

an even more forceful form, as with this prayer from the Liturgy of Malabar:

> Holy art thou, God, the Father of Truth, from whom all fatherhood in heaven and on earth is named; holy also is thine Only Begotten Son, our Lord Jesus Christ, by whom all things were made; holy also is the Spirit, the giver of all truth, by whom all are sanctified.[24]

This approach to blessing, in terms of holiness and being set apart, is a good and biblical one. The danger, perhaps, is to see blessing or consecration as a form of *withdrawal* from the world rather than as a prefiguration of the *redemption* of that world. Unless one has a particularly severe attachment to double predestination, we will understand the will of God as being for *all things* to be set apart, consecrated, made holy, conformed to him, and not simply some.[25] Blessing is a sign of the redemption of all things, not the damnation of most. Moreover, blessing or consecration should not be seen as some form of confiscation of things from themselves, some alienation from their own nature. Rather, blessing seeks to make things even more what they are and are called to be. That is part of what any proper account of redemption means. A blessed relationship, with its lifelong commitment, enters most fully into what a human relationship can be and mean; blessing a home commits us to all the virtues of homeliness; the chalice is the truest cup.

As a mental exercise, we can approach this through the question of what it means for something to be good. The tendency today is to see 'good' as primarily a moral term

---

24 Evelyn Underhill, *Eucharistic Prayers from the Ancient Liturgies* (London and New York: Longmans, Green & Co., 1939), p. 71.

25 Consider 1 Timothy 2.4; 2 Peter 3.9; Ephesians 1.10; Colossians 1.20.

and therefore to see goodness as primarily moral goodness. This is important, but theologians have not tended to
view moral goodness as the fundamental meaning of goodness. Pride of place, instead, has gone to something with
the potentially intimidating title of 'ontological goodness'.
This is simply the good of *being* – the good of being what
one is, and being it well. It is the goodness that we can
ascribe to an apple when we say that it is a 'good apple',
whereas it would make no sense to say that an apple was
morally good, or morally bad for that matter. 'Good' said
of an apple means that the apple lives up to what an apple
can be, while 'bad' said of an apple means a failure to be
well what it has been given for an apple to be.

There is a certain innocent simplicity to this sense of an
apple's goodness. The apple does not have to try hard to be
good in this way. That gives us a useful angle on the goodness of God, which is supremely a matter of no labour at
all. God's goodness consists far more in the plenitudinous
goodness of the boundlessness of his self-subsistent being
than it does in moral goodness. As David Bentley Hart puts
it, 'God is not some gentleman or lady out there in the great
beyond who happens to have a superlatively good character, but is a very ontological substance of goodness.'[26]

Holiness possesses a kinship to goodness, in this sense
most of all. While the goodness that most readily springs
to mind in this relation is moral goodness, we ought not
to forget the place of that 'ontological' goodness when it
comes to holiness. If we bless a building we are not so much
making it *morally* good as first of all affirming the 'ontological goodness' of its being. Then, we are praying that it
might embody its state as a building in a fulsome way. If,

---

26 David Bentley Hart, *The Experience of God: Being, Consciousness,
Bliss* (New Haven, CT: Yale University Press, 2013), pp. 253–4.

for instance, it is a church building, then we are asking God to make it the truest home of all: 'a house of God'. Blessing is by no means invoked to rarefy things, abstracting them from concrete existence and function. We bless a church not in order, somehow, to *overcome* its creaturely existence, in matter and time, in bricks and concrete, in angles and planes, but to affirm the goodness of that existence and perhaps in some sense to intensify it, since what is linked to Christ is linked to abundance.[27] A blessing does have some redemptive reference, and necessarily so, as we have seen, but we are not redeeming someone *from* being a human being or a relationship *from* being a human relationship or a thing *from* being a thing or a place *from* being a place. We are asking God to bring his redemption to bear so that creation may be redeemed from all that holds it back from being God's creation.

This brings us to the proposal, which is a common theme in writing on this topic, that all blessings should, in some sense, be seen as related to the blessing of bread and wine in the Eucharist. Gordon Lathrop puts it particularly well:

It is as if there are concentric circles of meaning around this central instance of Christian blessing. So we give thanks at our own table, blessing God over our good food, experiencing our meals as blessed, as little images of the Lord's Supper and of the eschatological banquet, being formed ourselves to care for the hungry. So we give thanks over the water of baptism (the prayer at the font is a blessing), over the light of the candle at the Easter Vigil or of Evening Prayer, over candidates for ordination

---

27 Consider John 10.10; Colossians 2.9.

(the ordination prayer is a blessing), over people who are affirming baptism, and also over oil and ashes.[28]

Alexander Schmemann made a similar point about the Eucharist, as also about baptism, which we can therefore extend to thinking about other, lesser, blessings: 'Christ came not to replace "natural" matter with some "super-natural" and sacred matter, but to restore and to fulfil it as the means of communion with God.'[29] Consider that the 'holy water in Baptism, the bread and wine in the Eucharist, stand for, i.e. represent, the whole of creation, but creation as it will be at the end, when it will be consummated in God, when He will fill all things with Himself'.[30] By analogy, we should not think of the blessing of a marriage or of a nun or of a chalice – for all the restrictions that may bring – as being in any way an attenuation, but quite the opposite. In each of these cases we have something of the dynamics of the Eucharist where, as Underhill put it, God makes the humble elements of bread and wine:

> that which all creation should be; a sacrament of His life and love . . . When this redeeming and consecrating action is complete, and the whole creation is the vehicle of the Spirit, it will become a living Eucharist. So the Eastern Church, adoring the transforming power of God at work on the humble oblation of bread and wine, sees in this the sign of a cosmic mystery, the

---

28 Lathrop, *Holy Ground*, p. 86.

29 Alexander Schmemann, *For the Life of the World: Sacraments and Orthodoxy* (Crestwood, NY: St Vladimir's Seminary Press, 1974), p. 49. Quoted in Hans Boersma, *Heavenly Participation: The Weaving of a Sacramental Tapestry* (Grand Rapids, MI: Eerdmans, 2011), p. 9.

30 Schmemann, *For the Life of the World*, p. 49.

consummation of all things, the transfiguration of the world in Christ.[31]

Creation comes to us as God's good gift, and the Eucharist demonstrates that God does not distain to be present to and within it. The Eucharist shows us the abundance of God's blessing, but we might also note the significance that the means of God's communication are humble elements: bread and wine. It is to the relation of those aspects – abundance and humility – that we now turn as we consider the 'prosperity gospel'.

31 Evelyn Underhill, *Mystery of Sacrifice*, p. 44. See also Olivier Clément, *On Human Being: A Spiritual Anthropology* (New York: New City Press, 2000), p. 116.

3

The 'Prosperity Gospel'

Blessing is related to vocation, or calling, and the call of God is to abundant life. Over the past century the connection of blessing to material abundance has been a theme of enormous significance within Christianity, in the form of the 'prosperity gospel'. This movement, phenomenon or mindset, has been widespread in Protestant Christianity and especially in Pentecostal Protestant Christianity. A contemporary historian of the movement, Kate Bowler, describes it as 'a wildly popular Christian message of spiritual, physical, and financial mastery that dominates not only much of the American religious scene but some of the largest churches around the globe'.[1] Its unifying themes, in the words of Bowler, are 'faith, wealth, health, and victory'.[2] In one recent survey, 17 per cent of Americans identified themselves as part of this movement and 31 per cent subscribed to the position that giving to church results in the blessing of a larger income.[3] We see the influence of the prosperity gospel most prominently in 'non-denominational' churches, although it is not

---

1 Kate Bowler, *Blessed: A History of the American Prosperity Gospel* (New York: Oxford University Press, 2013), p. 3.

2 Bowler, *Blessed*, p. 8.

3 Bowler, *Blessed*, p. 6. The poll is described as having been carried out shortly before the publication of the book (it is 'recent'), but no exact date is given.

only found there, and the congregations that draw heavily on this tradition can be both small and very large.[4]

As a starting place for evaluating the prosperity gospel message we might note just how much it resembles the religious scene into which the Christian message arrived: it promises prosperity and health in this world and does so in rather a pragmatic way, resembling what we would commonly call 'good luck'; for all its interest in material provision here and now it can be combined with an oth-erworldly view of salvation for some future life, and often is; the focus is largely on the prosperity of the individual or household, although with some sense that this can be sought within the context of a religious community; it is theologi-cally and philosophically syncretistic, while also distancing itself from highbrow theology and philosophy, and from the 'established' religion of the surrounding culture. In each of these ways, the prosperity gospel phenomenon aligns with the popular religious culture to be found across the Roman Empire when the Christian gospel was first announced.

Bowler situates the roots of the movement in America after the Civil War, in a period that is often called the 'gilded age'. Its intellectual groundwork is found as much *outside* the orthodox and biblical Christian tradition as within it. Especially influential were a cluster of ideas – often described today as the 'New Thought' – that placed great confidence in the power of the mind. As an example, consider Mary Baker Eddy and her 'Christian Science' movement, which so exalted mind above matter as to see the tangible world as all but illusory, suffering included.[5]

A more distinctly Christian contribution to the New Thought comes from E. W. Kenyon. His approach can to

---

4 Bowler, *Blessed*, p. 4.
5 Bowler, *Blessed*, pp. 12–15.

some extent be considered as a Christian reaction to the New Thought but in other ways it was continuous with it. He advocated what theologians would call a 'strongly realized eschatology', which is to say a sense that the coming kingdom of Christ had very significantly already arrived. That bolstered a strong expectation of healing. Kenyon's confidence in the power of words in bringing this about was to be a continuing feature of later prosperity gospel practice.[6]

Kenyon drew many of his ideas from biblical texts, approached superficially, but as a Christian vision of the world his picture was deficient. Rather in keeping with the New Thought after all was his sense that the Christian can have power over the material world because materiality means inferiority. On this view, worldly success could be expected or even demanded by the spiritual person: being spiritual, he or she is above the material world. The world's order, because of that, is not to be celebrated and engaged with according to its own form and logic but rather to be manipulated, using words that have power precisely because they belong to a 'higher', spiritual realm. Both the idea that the material world can be manipulated using techniques based on words and the supposed superiority of spiritual power over debased matter are suspiciously close to magic, and any such tendency to denigrate materiality has been labelled by the Church as 'Gnostic' and condemned accordingly. In keeping with the all but magical attitude here, Bowler points to some early influences on the prosperity gospel from Voodoo and associated practices.[7]

---

6 This can include belief in the power of efficacious 'prophetic' pronouncements, mysticism towards Hebrew names for God and invocation of the name of Jesus. Shorn of a debased connection to financial success, the latter two points find parallels in the history of Christian spirituality.

7 Bowler, *Blessed*, pp. 25–30.

The message, in short, was one of 'mind over matter'. This emphasis on the power of the mind and of well-chosen words was reinvigorated in the twentieth century, with a psychological spin, by Norman Vincent Peale (1898–1993) and his 'power of positive thinking'. Another important influence was a consistent emphasis within Reformed Protestantism of the goodness of capitalism and the godliness of hard work.[8] To this day, 'The prosperity gospel's emphasis on the individual's responsibility for his or her own fate resonated strongly with the American tradition of rugged self-reliance.'[9]

Perhaps the decisive figure for the prosperity gospel as we might encounter it today is Granville Oral Roberts. His life, he said, was changed by reading the second verse of John's Third Epistle: 'Beloved, I wish above all things that thou mayest prosper and be in health, even as thy soul prospereth' (in the Authorized Version, as he would have read it). Roberts described this verse as 'the greatest discovery I ever made' and as the foundation for all that he went on to do,[10] although he also liked to draw attention to Luke 6.38:

Give, and it shall be given unto you; good measure, pressed down, and shaken together, and running over, shall men give into your bosom. For with the same measure that ye mete withal it shall be measured to you again. (AV)

---

8 Here Russell H. Conwell (1843–1925) is particularly significant. See Bowler, *Blessed*, pp. 31–2.

9 Bowler, *Blessed*, p. 227.

10 Oral Roberts and Eloise Gray, *Oral Roberts' Life Story* (Tulsa, OK: Oral Roberts Evangelist Association, 1952), pp. 70–5. Quoted by Bowler, *Blessed*, p. 49. It was published in 1952, and 'the first of many' autobiographies, as Bowler puts it – *Blessed*, p. 49.

Our response to the figure of Roberts can stand for a response to the prosperity movement as a whole. As a first move, we should not be so quick to dismiss either him or it. He was inspired by 3 John 2, and why not be so inspired? John's desire – or the desire of the author of the letter that bears his name – was that his readers might 'prosper and be in health'. In Luke 6, Jesus did indeed promise a full measure in return for what is given. These texts are in the Scriptures and we must take them seriously. In doing that, it would be illegitimate to 'spiritualize' the desires that these passages address, passing over any bodily, this-worldly reference. Christianity is the religion of creation, the incarnation and the physical resurrection, of the naked clothed and the hungry fed, not of disembodied spirits. In any case, taken in its broadest terms, extensive research has shown that religious practice *does* correlate with indices of mental and physical health, happiness and longevity.[11]

We cannot be dismissive of the physical and material reference in passages such as these. On the other hand, the desire for prosperity and health in 3 John goes hand in hand with a desire for prosperity of soul: 'even as thy soul prospereth', as Roberts' favourite verse concludes. Neither 3 John nor any tradition in subsequent mainstream Christianity would advise us to seek material prosperity in any way that leads to a malady of the soul. Unfortunately, just such a malady is to be found in the work and teaching of Granville Oral Roberts. He became famous for promising a miraculous financial return on gifts made to him, with a focus on a sevenfold increase,[12] and for threatening his followers that if they did not donate a certain phenom-

---

11 See H. G. Koenig, D. E. King and V. B. Carson (eds), *Handbook of Religion and Health*, 2nd edn (New York: Oxford University Press, 2012).

12 Bowler, *Blessed*, p. 49

enal amount God would kill him (or 'call him home').[13] According to one report at his death, he asked staff to air-brush his diamond rings from publicity pictures.[14]

When prosperity teachers came to discuss blessing in terms of material abundance, they had much to go on. Their fault was not in pointing to prosperity in the Bible but rather in failing to point to the whole of the biblical witness. They failed to hold the material that promises prosperity in tension with other material that deals – with searing realism – with the observation that the righteous do not always flourish. Nor did they appreciate how much the Bible and the Christian theological tradition had reframed blessedness beyond material success – but not entirely in isolation from it. They forgot that the Son of Man had nowhere to lay his head (Matt. 8.20; Luke 9.58). Similarly, while the phrase 'strive first for the kingdom of God and his righteousness, and all these things will be given to you as well' (Matt. 6.33; Luke 12.31) does indeed place more of an emphasis on 'things' than is sometimes acknowledged, to set our heart primarily on these 'things' would clearly be to turn the passage on its head.

All this said, Roberts can appear as a moderate figure among prosperity preachers, compared to some who came after. We might consider Frederick J. Eikerenkoetter and his shocking inversion of 1 Timothy 6.10: 'the lack of money is the root of all evil'.[15] Then there are the televangelists Jim and Tammy Faye Bakker, who made lavish financial demands on their followers and put the money

---

13 Obituary, *Guardian*, 15 December 2009; *The Economist*, 30 December 2009.

14 Obituary, *Daily Telegraph*, 16 December 2009.

15 Quoted by Bowler, *Blessed*, p. 67, citing David Edwin Harrell, *All Things Are Possible: The Healing and Charismatic Revivals in Modern America* (Bloomington, IN: Indiana University Press, 1975), p. 23.

to use on an equally lavish lifestyle. They used the spectacle of their own fur-lined affluence as confirmation of the maxim that God rewards with worldly success those who are faithful to him – their followers had only to believe as hard as they did (and keep giving). Eventually, however, their religious, media and property empire collapsed; the couple divorced and Jim Bakker was sentenced to 40 years in prison on a number of charges related to fraud (reduced to eight years in resentencing). He denied accusations of rape but admitted having sexual intercourse with a church worker.[16] It was a very undignified collapse of a Christian ministry.

Looking at the movement as a whole, Bowler draws a distinction between 'soft' and 'hard' prosperity preaching. The 'soft' version sees faith as the *cure* for material need; the 'hard' version goes further, seeing lack of faith as the *cause* of material need. Bowler paints a picture of a 'hard' prosperity church service that can only fittingly be called grotesque:

Prosperity congregations, unable to find sufficient precedent in . . . [existing] church practices, developed modern rites to celebrate divine wealth on Sunday morning . . . [Several trends emerged.] Tithing eclipsed the sermon, worship, and communion as the emotional peak of the service, as pastors pushed their audiences to envision greater financial miracles. Soft prosperity churches commonly kept the mood light as the ushers took the offering, reminding audiences 'God loves a cheerful giver' (2 Cor. 9.7). Hard prosperity congregations adopted stronger measures, dwelling on the negative consequences that befell the uncharitable. In the book of

---

16 Jim Bakker, *I Was Wrong* (Nashville, TN: Nelson, 1998).

Malachi, teachers found ample evidence that Christians cursed themselves when they 'robbed God'.[17]

Pressure, as she relates, can often be 'unsubtle': 'Pastors might ask congregants to turn to their neighbors in the pew and inquire: "Did you give what you were supposed to?" and to tell any reluctant givers, "I'm not going to sit by you if you're not here for victory!"'[18]

This movement is easy to criticize, and much of that criticism is necessary and just. For all that, we should also recognize that the movement is anything but uniform and that the good and bad are often found close together within it. Even figures whose theology we might want to reject as highly suspect could act in highly commendable ways when it came to certain practical questions. An example would be Carlton Pearson, whose work for racial integration in the United States was far ahead of his time,[19] or Father Divine, who was concerned with bettering the prospects of the black poor almost half a century earlier.[20]

The attention of members of these churches to worldly success, even obsession, may strike us as unattractive or unchristian, and I am far from recommending its excesses. However, we might do well to consider who it is who finds these congregations so attractive: they are the poor and those whose opportunities are limited and few. As a salutary lesson on this front, I remember delivering a lecture on the doctrine of God in which I expressed my strongly held conviction that divine omnipotence should not be considered as the principal divine attribute (although it often has since the early fourteenth

---

17 Bowler, *Blessed*, p. 128. The whole of her 'Sunday Prosperity' section (pp. 127–34) merits attention.

18 Bowler, *Blessed*, p. 130.

19 Bowler, *Blessed*, p. 91.

20 Bowler, *Blessed*, p. 28.

century). I gave the example of a church I had once passed, rooted in the prosperity tradition, which I remembered (or misremembered) as being called 'His Tabernacle of Power'. How odd, I remarked, that anyone would want to single out this attribute, power, in the name of their church. 'Not so odd', came the reply, from a black student, 'if the congregation came from families that had been all but powerless for generations.' Her point was well made. No one in poverty need think that God is ambivalent to their suffering or wishes anyone to sit tight in meek expectation of a better life to come after death. Theological criticisms of the prosperity gospel are not difficult to make and in their own way they are entirely necessary, but such criticisms only ring fully true if those who make them are also willing to play their part in the Church's work to alleviate poverty. We should indeed find something both skewed and missing in Kenneth Copeland's quip that a 'Gospel to the poor' simply means that 'Jesus has come and they don't need to be poor anymore!'[21] It would, however, be equally skewed to suppose that Christ or his Church are oblivious to material suffering. For all its faults, many have found in the prosperity movement an affirmation that it is not the business of the faith to 'keep them under'. The prosperity gospel movement is least askew when it lines up with the basic human desire for the necessities of life, for oneself and for those under one's care; it is most askew when it substitutes luxury for holiness and invests itself in the abstraction of money rather than in the more tangible and substantial goods of human life.

While plenty of prosperity congregations live up to the caricature of a focus on miraculous deliverance, 'earned' by sacrificial donations that have been offered on the basis

---

21 Kenneth Copeland, *Prosperity: The Choice is Yours* (Fort Worth, TX: KCP Publications, 1985), p. 10.

of a careful calculus of returns, others – albeit to vary-
ing degrees – have placed a parallel emphasis on practical
responses to poverty, not least through programmes of education.[22] In the USA this has been particularly prominent
among African American churches (not least among those
with strong connections with the historic denominations),
where attention has often been given to entrepreneurialism
and associated practical skills. Bowler lists debt counselling,
instruction on tax write-offs, job banks and small business
loans. More than the quick-fix variety, these churches are
likely to sense that the 'slow work of upward mobility' is
a gradual process and that aspirations for 'overnight success' do not make good business sense (whatever theological sense they may or may not make).[23] In the best of
this movement we might even detect a concern for human
excellence that bears comparison with the 'virtue' tradition
in Christian ethics, even if it might simultaneously suffer
from an unreflective adherence to contemporary cultural
assumptions as to what makes for a good life.

Who is Blessed?

To place the prosperity urge within a wider theological
framework, part of the task will be to reiterate a point
that has already been made in this book: that blessing is
not simply a celebration of the abundance of creation or a
prayer for a share in the abundance but also an acknowledgement of fallenness – both in the world around us and
within ourselves – and a matter of calling upon God to rem-
edy that situation. We have also seen that blessing always
lives alongside elements of consecration. Elements of giving

---

22 For examples, see Bowler, *Blessed*, pp. 27–8, 91–2, 115.
23 Bowler, *Blessed*, p. 126.

up and of dedication to a particular purpose or way of life are part of the picture of blessing and of a proper sense of abundance, and not simply the arithmetic of endless multiplication. This chimes with any sensible analysis of what makes for human contentedness.[24]

Pressing a little further, a response to the excesses of the prosperity gospel can come by reframing the question, asking 'Who, exactly, is blessed?' Who is it that the biblical witness tends to hold up as particularly a recipient of divine blessing? Turning our attention to the New Testament, a concordance yields a striking list. The blessed are those who live by the beatitudes: 'the poor in spirit', 'those who mourn', 'the meek', 'those who hunger and thirst for righteousness', 'the merciful', 'the pure in heart', 'the peacemakers' and 'those who are persecuted for righteousness' sake' (Matt. 5.3–10). Christ amplified that last point: 'Blessed are you when people revile you and persecute you and utter all kinds of evil against you falsely on my account' (Matt. 5.11). We find similar themes in the Letter of James: the blessed are those who have endured trials (James 1.12; 5.11). In

---

24 On a simple human level, without any necessary consideration of theology, the question of what makes for human happiness has become a significant topic of discussion in recent years. For a survey, see Richard Layard, *Happiness: Lessons from a New Science* (London: Penguin, 2011). One important component is purposeful work, by which we *make* something, however broadly we might interpret that term. That might be for leisure as much as for livelihood; indeed, it is particularly associated with leisure. On this, see Richard Sennett, *The Craftsman* (London: Penguin Books, 2009). This accords with the biblical sense that human blessedness is aligned with some sort of creative engagement with the material world, the paradigm being growing crops and domesticating the earth rather than accumulating surplus wheat in barns; fashioning items out of gold for the praise of God rather than labouring to be able to store golden coins in a vault. These reflections, ostensibly 'non-theological' though they may be, can be part of a productive Christian reflection on what makes for a good and blessed life. Layard, Sennett and others have things to teach every overly busy Christian seeking to make an ascetic journey.

John's Gospel we read 'Blessed also are those who have not seen, and yet believe' (John 20.29) and, in Luke, 'Blessed . . . are those who hear the word of God and obey it' (Luke 11.28). In that passage, the comment bears a *structural* contrast with the Virgin Mary:

> a woman in the crowd raised her voice and said to him, 'Blessed is the womb that bore you and the breasts that nursed you!' But he said, 'Blessed rather are those who hear the word of God and obey it!' (Luke 11.27–28)

In reality, however, we have not a contrast but an alignment, since Mary is herself a paradigm of blessedness precisely as one who heard the word of God and obeyed it. Remaining with Mary, we might suggest three foundations for her blessedness: first because of God's undeserved favour or grace ('Greetings, favoured one!'); second because of the role that she is to be given in God's plan; and third because she is obedient to God's call: 'Here am I, the servant of the Lord; let it be with me according to your word' (Luke 1.26–38). We should not miss the connection between these observations – we should not separate Mary's response from God's grace as if she, or any of us, act independently of the grace of God in which we stand; nor does her role in salvation stand disconnected from her choice as if she were merely a puppet. In God's grace all of these things coinhere.

Mary is the supremely blessed human being (if, for the moment, we choose not to speak of Christ in those terms): the woman who was above all called to 'hear and obey' the word of God. As an Orthodox anthem puts it, she was given the task of making answer for all of creation to the redeeming will of God. Moreover, if, rightly, we call Mary holy, that is not *primarily* because she was an especially 'good person'. The central meaning is that she was so significantly *set aside* for a particular task: 'Light, fire and life, divine and immortal, / Joined to our nature you have brought forth', as that Orthodox anthem puts it.[25] Holiness and blessedness, here, are primarily to be understood in terms of consecration to her task.

Soon after the Annunciation in Luke's account, the Holy Family are *blessed* by the priest Simeon, as we have seen. To that blessing Simeon adds some words:

> This child is destined for the falling and the rising of many in Israel, and to be a sign that will be opposed so that the inner thoughts of many will be revealed – and a sword will pierce your own soul too. (Luke 2.34–35)

The blessedness present here is anything but glib. We are left with no illusions as to what it will cost.

As a final paradigmatic example of what it means to be blessed from a New Testament perspective, we might consider this passage from Mark:

> Peter began to say to him, 'Look, we have left everything and followed you.' Jesus said, 'Truly I tell you, there is no one who has left house or brothers or sisters or mother or father or children or fields, for my sake and for the sake of the good news, who will not receive a hundredfold now in this age – houses, brothers and sisters, mothers and children, and fields, with persecutions – and in the age to come eternal life. (Mark 10.28–30)[26]

---

25 Translated by the Sisters of West Malling.
26 The parallels are Matthew 19.27–29 and Luke 18.28–30, both of which lack 'with persecutions'.

Here we have sacrifice – all that Peter and Christians down the ages have given up – but it is not presented as sacrifice in any futile sense, as sacrifice simply for the sake of loss. To the embarrassment of any such tragic vision, those who give any of these things up are promised *a hundredfold* in return, and not only deferred to some future age but 'now in this age'. What is more, they receive eternal life, and this is not offered as an alternative to that hundredfold now. And yet in contrast to any easy 'prosperity' interpretation of this passage, we should note what Mark intersperses among those 'houses, brothers and sisters, fields' and so on: the words 'with persecutions'. This is no recipe for an easy ride.

We might still wonder just what it means to receive a hundredfold return of houses or fields, in this life, or of brothers and sisters, mothers and children, for that matter. My sense is that it revolves around incorporation into the Church. The Christian *receives* all of these goods a hundredfold because they are *received* into the Church. Within the body of the Church they have all of these things, but as a common good, not as a possession: they do not *own* any of this hundredfold increase in 'fields', not in the sense of arrogating them to themselves. What Christians hold, they hold in trust, as a gift out of which they can provide for the needs of others. We might think of the example of Acts 4.24–47 where, in fact, a field is mentioned.

Mark's passage points to several of the central features of blessedness within the Christian tradition, especially when held alongside that passage from Acts: part of what we receive 'in return' is a sense of purpose – a duty towards 'brothers and sisters, mothers and children' – and the ownership of what we own (in a light sense of that word) is similarly given purpose: within the household of the Church, the needs (although not luxuries) of all are to be cared for.

The logic is one of abundance and not of paucity; the focus is more on persons than things: new prominence is given to personal and relational ways of speaking (brothers and sisters, mother, father and children), and if 'objects' are still spoken of, such as 'houses' and 'fields', then, we might also note, these are items that undergird communal life rather than substitutes for it.

Today, no doubt, most Christians have a less lively sense than those first believers of the supreme gift – the blessedness – of having a place within the community of the Church. Perhaps we experience some of these features but take them for granted: simply belonging to a community might seem unremarkable, even belonging to a community where the care of one by another has a prominent place. The reader may, in this, not know how fortunate he or she really is or, to use a better word, how blessed. From my own perspective, I have felt the force of this passage from Mark most profoundly when I have been travelling. Travel can provide a vivid sense of belonging, in the Church, to a family that spans the globe. Certainly, in this way, I have been aware just how much I have received a hundredfold of houses, brothers and sisters, mothers, fathers and children, and fields.

As a final point we might notice a strange conjunction, which is nonetheless distinctively Christian: that blessedness is both tough and cheerful. Blessed are the poor in spirit, or even – in Luke – simply the poor; blessed are the meek and those who are persecuted for righteousness' sake; blessed is she whose soul was pierced by a sword of sorrow. Abundance may come, but 'with persecutions'. And yet abundance *is* promised all the same, and if we look at those fearsome beatitudes we find that the word usually translated as 'blessed' is *makarios*. Its meaning shades into being favoured and indeed into being *happy*.

Some teasing out might be necessary here. English, which is usually so well provided with words, nonetheless uses one word here ('blessed') to refer to two distinct but related ideas. One set bears most directly upon having been blessed; in Latin this would be *benedictus*, as at the beginning of the canticle that bears that name: 'Blessed be the Lord God of Israel; for he hath visited and redeemed his people' (Luke 1.68, AV). The other set of ideas are what the beatitudes refer to: that sense of being happy, favoured or complete. The Latin here is *beatus* for men – so that Psalm 1 begins *Beatus vir* – or *beata* for women.[27] If we really wanted to distinguish these ideas in English we could make use of our slightly archaic word 'beatitude' (for being happy, favoured or complete). All the same, a hard and fast distinction between 'beatitude' and 'having been blessed' may not be necessary. For one thing, while a parallel distinction in Hebrew is recognizable, it can be overstated. (It is between *'ashrè*, as at the opening of Psalm 1, and *barak*, the more usual word for blessing.[28]) The Virgin Mary, for example, is described in both ways, as both *benedicta* (having been blessed), as in Luke 1.28 (and the prayer Hail Mary, which comes from it), and as *beata* (blessed, happy), as in her standard Latin title *Beata Virgo Maria* (Blessed Virgin Mary).

---

27 In standard Roman Catholic usage, 'blessed' (*beatus* or *beata*) is used as the title of someone 'halfway' to sainthood: someone who has been 'beatified' but not 'canonized'. In a book on blessing we might note with some satisfaction that 'blessedness' is not *always* seen as halfway to holiness. In the ancient Western Eucharistic Prayer (the 'Roman Canon', in the prayer *Confiteor*), the principal saints are called 'blessed', before moving on to others who are given the title of 'saint': *Confiteor Deo omnipotenti, beatæ Mariæ semper Virgini, beato Michaeli Archangelo, beato Ioanni Baptistæ, sanctis Apostolis Petro et Paulo, omnibus Sanctis . . .*

28 Joseph Auneau, 'Blessing – A Biblical Theology', in Jean-Yves Lacoste ed., *Encyclopedia of Christian Theology* (London: Routledge, 2004), p. 218.

Rather than lamenting the rather blunt alignment of these two ideas in English, we can celebrate it as making a helpful link in both directions. On the one hand we can appreciate that all true happiness, contentment and fulfilment comes to us from God, as God's blessing. On the other we see that the ultimate effect of God's grace or blessing, whatever the cost might be on the way, is happiness and abundance of life: we need not be ashamed that we want to be happy, although we are certainly likely to need some education from the tradition as to what the truest happiness looks like.

On this territory, Christian ethics has long found common cause with a tradition that finds a particularly eloquent expression in Aristotle (among other ancient philosophers), often called *eudaimonistic* ethics.[29] This Greek word is difficult to translate but means something quite close to happiness-as-fulfilment. It teaches not only that the truest human achievement, and happiness, lies in doing what is right, but also – as a consequence – that the quest for such happiness, properly conceived, is a good moral guide. In English it often goes by the name of 'virtue ethics', the virtues being those dispositions of character that make for happy fulfilment. (Fulfilment here is just the right word: the sense is of something coming to 'fill out' all that it can be.[30]) Being blessed in the sense of *beatus* or *makarios* is very close to this idea.

---

29 See, for instance, Daniel C. Russell, 'Virtue Ethics, Happiness, and the Good Life', in Daniel C. Russell (ed.), *The Cambridge Companion to Virtue Ethics* (Cambridge: Cambridge University Press, 2013), pp. 7–28, along with other essays in that collection, and Jean Porter, 'Virtue Ethics', in Philip L. Quinn and Charles Taliaferro (eds), *A Companion to Philosophy of Religion* (Oxford: Blackwell, 1997), pp. 466–72.

30 I take this to be the sense with which the whole variety of creatures are exhorted to 'bless the Lord' in the *Benedicite*, as I mentioned in Chapter 1.

Blessing things – in the sense of *benedictio* – is not so far away either. We have seen that a blessing is an acknowledgement and an orientation to God. When we bless something, someone or somewhere, we are in some way pointing to what it can most truly be; we are directing it to its fulfilment in God. That is what lies at the heart of the connection between blessing and vocation, which is about discovering 'what you are for'. The Eucharistic Prayer, most of all blessings, deserves to be called a consecration, for all it goes beyond any other consecration in the extent to which it transforms what is blessed, and in it material elements are fulfilled: bread, in becoming the body of Christ, becomes the truest bread; wine, in becoming the blood of Christ, becomes the truest wine. In all of this Christ is central, and it is to him that we turn in our next chapter.

4

Christology: Jesus as the Son of the Blessed One

At the climax of Mark's account of the trial of Jesus, the high priest asks Jesus about his status in relation to God. 'Are you', the priest asks, 'the Messiah, the Son of the Blessed One?' 'I am', Jesus replies (Mark 14.61–62). The priest was asking Jesus whether he was the Son of God. We need not read too much into his precise turn of phrase: 'the Blessed One' is one of several standard circumlocutions for speaking about God, such as 'Most High'. Calling God the Blessed One is both an ascription of praise, along the lines we have already discussed, and a way to avoid mentioning the holy name of God itself. All the same, 'Son of the Blessed One' is an apt name for Jesus. As Son of the Blessed One, Jesus is supremely blessed himself. He is acclaimed as such both by Elizabeth ('Blessed are you [Mary] among women, and blessed is *the fruit of your womb*' – Luke 1.42) and by the crowd on Palm Sunday ('Blessed is the one who comes in the name of the Lord!' – Mark 11.9[1]).

The designation of Jesus as 'blessed' or the 'Son of the Blessed One' opens up several lines of theological discussion. For one thing, it is vital for Christian theology to say

---

1 With parallels in each of the other Gospels: Matthew 21.9; Luke 19.38; John 12.13.

that Jesus inherits and fulfils all of the blessings of God upon Israel. In Galatians, Paul links Christ with blessing as the one in whom the promises to Abraham are fulfilled (Gal. 3). In Romans he links all of the blessing upon Israel with Christ as the Messiah, adding what seems to be one of Paul's clearest ascriptions of deity to Christ in any of his letters, precisely using 'blessedness' language:

> to them belong the adoption, the glory, the covenants, the giving of the law, the worship, and the promises; to them belong the patriarchs, and from them, according to the flesh, comes the Messiah, who is over all, God blessed for ever. Amen. (Rom. 9.4–5)[2]

As one way to express this, the book of Acts records Paul as also seeing Christ as inheriting the blessings upon *David*: 'And as for the fact that he raised him from the dead, no more to return to corruption, he has spoken in this way, "I will give you the holy and sure blessings of David"' (Acts 13.34, ESV).

We should not think here that Jesus stands in for Israel, receiving these blessings instead of God's chosen people. Rather Jesus inherits and fulfils these blessings as the true Israelite. This goes hand in hand, as we might expect, with his inheriting and fulfilling the vocation of Israel: to be a light to the nations, for instance (Isa. 49.6; Luke 2.32). With this vocation comes all that it means to be conse-crated or set part for God, including, in this fallen world, the suffering that comes from being God's chosen one in a

---

2 We can note that one of the other passages in the Pauline corpus that might be read most straightforwardly as an ascription of deity to Christ again mentions blessedness: 'while we wait for the blessed hope and the manifestation of the glory of our great God and Saviour, Jesus Christ' (Titus 2.13).

world of sin. That was an element of what it meant to be the chosen people or a representative of the chosen people, which Second Isaiah was not slow to spell out in the Songs of the Suffering Servant.[3]

Blessing concerns life and abundance of life, and the affirmation or even intensification of the proper goodness of a thing, situation or person. Jesus is also blessed in this sense, being the perfect human being. The touchstone of orthodoxy when it comes to the Person of Christ, for both the Western Churches and the Eastern Orthodox Churches, is the declaration of the Council of Chalcedon. As it puts it, Christ is 'perfect in humanity'. The Greek, *teleion*, comes from the same root as the verb 'finished' in Christ's saying from the cross, 'It is finished' (John 19.30). As our use of the related Greek word *telos* implies, the sense is of something perfect, in the sense of having been completed or fulfilled. This is a necessary part of the background to the word that the Fathers of the Council of Chalcedon used to indicate the perfection both of Christ's divinity and of his humanity.

As they went on to say, Christ's divinity does not undo his humanity but establishes it in perfection. When Pilate displayed Christ to the people with the words 'Here is the man!' (John 19.4 – 'Behold the Man' in the AV), he did not appreciate how profoundly true his words were: there indeed, before them, was the full, perfect, axiomatic, emblematic human being, the one who teaches us what it means to be human. Jesus is perfectly good, again not just in the sense of moral goodness but also in that 'ontological' sense of filling out what a thing can be.

Understanding what it means for Christ to be blessed calls for a fully Trinitarian account. For one thing, Christ

---

3 Especially Isaiah 49.1–6; 50.4–9; 53.1–11.

is blessed as the perfect recipient of the Holy Spirit. He was divine in his very person, but he was also perfectly human, and being divine did not prevent him from relating to God in the way that any other human being relates, namely through the Spirit. Christ was the perfect recipient of the Spirit, the one upon whom the Spirit of the Lord 'rests' (Luke 4.18, quoting Isaiah 61.1).

The Spirit was always with Christ, since he was conceived by the power of the Spirit (Luke 1.35). All the same, we can see his baptism as a moment when the Spirit rested upon him to commission him for his ministry (Mark 1.10; Matt. 3.16; Luke 3.22; John 1.32). Alongside this descent of the Spirit, the voice of the Father was heard, announcing that Jesus is his 'beloved Son' in whom he is pleased (Mark 1.11; Matt. 3.17; Luke 3.22). The Dutch spiritual writer Henri Nouwen saw this as another element of blessing upon the person and work of Christ. 'Jesus is the Blessed One', he wrote, 'because God has spoken good things of him',[4] here picking up on the etymology of 'benediction'. 'Most clearly', Nouwen goes on,

> we hear God's blessing after Jesus has been baptized in the river Jordon, when 'suddenly there was a voice from heaven, "This is my Son, the Beloved, my favour rests on him."' With this blessing Jesus starts his public ministry. And all of that ministry makes known to us that this blessing is not only for Jesus but also for all who follow.

What we see to be true of Jesus in his earthly life gives us our best insight about the eternal nature of God. Just as

---

4 Henri Nouwen, *Bread for the Journey* (San Francisco: Harper, 1997), entry for May 22.

Christ is both supremely blessed, and this as something that he receives from God, so in the eternal life of the Trinity the Son of God is equal to the Father in blessedness and yet receives this from the Father. To be blessed is to receive the favour of God, and God's love and presence. The Son's entire being is the reception of the blessing of the Father.

The Son enters into blessings of Israel, and the vocation to be a blessing, and he does not keep that to himself. Rather his plan is to gather up 'all things' into his body, the Church, and into his 'inheritance' (Eph. 1). We see this link between Christ's vocation of blessing and ours spelt out particularly in 1 Peter, where the author urges his readers to bless those who do them ill: 'Do not repay evil for evil or abuse for abuse; but, on the contrary, repay with a blessing. It is for this that you were called – that you might inherit a blessing' (1 Pet. 3.9).

This places good and evil before us, and the triumph of blessing over curse. These are the themes to which we turn in the next chapter.

5

Sin: Curses, Cursing and their Abolition

Blessing is associated with cursing as up is associated with down and gain with loss. A discussion of curses in a book on blessing might, therefore, be included simply as an exercise in completeness, but there is more to it than that. In its way, this book offers a brisk trawl through some of the topics of systematic theology, approached from the perspective of blessing: creation, the doctrine of God and so on. Taken with cursing, blessing bears upon the doctrine of redemption. We need to have a proper sense of what we are redeemed *from* in order to understand what we mean by salvation (although with the caveat that just as much attention should be given to what we are saved *for* or *to* as what we are saved *from*). One theological answer is that we are redeemed from a curse. That answer means that this chapter is therefore no interlude in a book on blessing, not least since *all* Christian blessings are, to some degree, understood within the wider picture of redemption.

Blessing and cursing obviously belong together as opposite words or antonyms. In another sense they have a closer association still. The words 'bless' and 'curse' are surprisingly interwoven, both in current practice and in ancient literature, the Bible included. An example comes in the book of Job, where Job's wife urges him to capitulate to his calamity: 'bless God and die', she suggests (Job 2.9). The verb here is from the standard Hebrew verb for blessing, *barak*. The sense is possibly that Job should 'bless' God, in the sense of praising him, and then hope to die in peace. That, however, sits at odds with the logic of the story and with the general tenor of the advice Job is receiving from his wife. Few Bible translations, in fact, render the text this way: 'bless God and die'.[1] More likely, the biblical scholars tell us, the sense is what might seem like the very opposite – '*curse* God and die'. Cursing God will provoke a wrathful response from God and therefore bring on Job's death: 'Get it over with', Job's wife is suggesting. Perhaps that is how the Hebrew originally stood, and at some point a scribe altered 'curse' to 'bless', either as a knowing euphemism for the horrible injunction to curse God or as a veil to hide that terrible suggestion from impressionable hearers. Or maybe it was always written as 'bless God', in that euphemistic way. The same transposition is found in Job 1.5, where the literal wording of 'blessed God in their hearts' means 'cursed God in their hearts'. One way or another, blessing and cursing are strangely interrelated in this book.

Although writing 'bless' when we mean 'curse' might seem odd, it is not such a surprising inversion. In the ancient Greek world the word *sacer* meant 'sacred' (indeed, it is the root of that English word). The idea is clearly closely related to blessing but it could also mean something very much like 'cursed'. The *homo sacer* – the 'consecrated person' – occupied a position similar to that of the sacrificial victim

---

[1] The Douay-Rheims translation does. It, however, is a translation of the Latin Vulgate, not of the Hebrew, and the Vulgate retains the reference to blessing: *benedic Deo et morere*. The Septuagint, the ancient Greek translation of the Old Testament, is more elliptical: 'say some word to [*or* against] the Lord, and die'. The preposition *eis* is a little ambiguous, perhaps deliberately so, but *against* seems the most reasonable translation.

(and again, *sacer* is the root of the English word 'sacrifice').[2] James Frazer made a great deal of the suggestion that the figure of the consecrated and cursed king lay at the heart of much ancient Greek myth, and the theme was taken up by Robert Graves.[3] We see this negative connotation of the word *sacer* in Virgil when he talks of the 'accursed' (*sacra*) human love of wealth, even to their own destruction.[4] We find a similar conjunction in the Old Testament command to set apart the spoils of war for dedication to God. The Hebrew is *hērem*, and that dedication is also a vow of destruction (e.g. Num. 21.2; Josh. 6.19; 1 Sam. 15.8, 15).[5]

In present-day usage, or at least in recent usage, the adjective *blessed* has been used to mean something like 'damned'. This was my paternal grandmother's most frequent expression of disapprobation: 'this blessed thing',

---

2 René Girard has written about the 'sacred' but excluded and damned figure, for instance in *Violence and the Sacred* (London: Routledge, 2005). John Milbank has written about Christ as the *homo sacer*, whereby he occupied this role so as to put an end to the futility of sacrifice – *Being Reconciled* (London: Routledge, 2003), pp. 79–93.

3 James George Frazer, *The Golden Bough: A Study in Magic and Religion* (London: Macmillan, 1911); Robert Graves, *The White Goddess: A Historical Grammar of Poetic Myth* (London: Faber & Faber, 1961).

4 'To what crime do you not drive the hearts of men, accursed hunger for gold' (*quid non mortalia pectora cogis, auri sacra fames?*), *Aeneid*, trans. H. R. Fairclough; rev. C. P. Goold (Cambridge: Loeb, 1999), III.56–7, p. 376 for Latin, p. 377 for English.

5 The idea is likely to be ethically problematic for the contemporary reader. John Howard Yoder pointed out that the proper background for understanding the novelty of the idea is one of even greater violence. Against that background, the idea of *hērem* functions as a principle of restraint: extreme violence was taken as a given at that time; *hērem* prevented conquest from being a vehicle for 'immediate enrichment through plunder' – 'If Abraham Is Our Father', in *The Original Revolution: Essays on Christian Pacifism* (Scottdale, PA: Herald Press, 1971; repr. Wipf & Stock), p. 105. We need not think that *hērem* is the last word in the ethics of war. Ethical thinking would go further but, for its time, this idea stood as a commandment of restraint.

said perhaps of a misbehaving kitchen appliance, was not an ascription of honour. As yet another example of the relation between blessing and curse, consider also how we characteristically make swear words or 'curse words' from the realm of that which we find most sacred – typically from a religious setting, as when the name of Jesus is used as an expletive, or from a sexual setting (with the reader open to imagine his or her own examples). For an example of this principle at work we can notice that sexual swear words are common in Continental French speech, where – we might venture – such sexual concerns presently carry greater weight than religious ones. French Canada, however, remained far more devout than France (until the 1960s). As a result, swear words in Canadian French are frequently taken from the realm of Catholic sacramental piety, for which there is little direct parallel in Europe. Examples include *tabarnac* (tabernacle, where the Blessed Sacrament is stored), *sacrament*, *câlice* (chalice) and *ciboire* (ciborium, the vessel of consecrated bread).[6] The territory of the most sacred and blessed provides the repository from which we typically draw words for cursing.

As a final example of the blessing–cursing ambiguity, consider the word reserved by the ancient councils of the Church for their most severe denunciation: *anathema*. We think of the ancient councils as having produced statements of doctrine, such as the Nicene Creed (which actually evolved over two councils), as indeed they did. Just as common, and even more so, were lists of 'anathemas' condemning particular heresies. These anathemas we typically expressed in a form such as 'Should anyone say *x*, let that person be accursed [literally, in Latin, *anathema sit*].'

---

6 I had a helpful discussion of this topic with Jacob Sherman, for which I am most grateful.

Anathema here means accursed, 'cut off' or excluded. By pronouncing an anathema, a council declared some doctrinal position to be off limits (such as saying that Jesus was not fully human or not fully divine), and as a consequence, anyone holding that position was similarly 'off limits', excluded from the body of the Church.[7]

Linguistically, the word anathema – this most solemn of curses – was originally a word for blessing, in the sense of consecration. The Greek is derived from *ana* ('up') and *tithenai* ('to put'), and originally referred to something dedicated to a god by being hung up in a temple, by way of thanks. (Hanging up offerings in this way, as an ex-voto, is still common in Roman Catholic churches in Continental Europe.) This sense, close to the etymology of the word, is the way it is used in Luke 21.5: 'some were speaking about the temple, how it was *adorned* with beautiful stones and gifts dedicated to God'. The word, then, started out related to blessing and thanks but, in parallel to what we have already seen, anathema later came to mean something cursed and cut off from God (as in Rom. 9.3; 1 Cor. 12.3; 16.22; Gal. 1.8, 9). It is the Greek word used to translate that Hebrew word for consecration-as-destruction: *hērem*. As one dictionary puts it, 'because it was associated with setting apart (for God), it gradually came to have the meaning as set apart (from God)'.[8]

Seeing an anathema as a cutting off provides a helpful reminder that the truest meaning of a curse is some form of exclusion: it breaks off a relationship. A curse is an estrangement. In British life, although happily not often today, this found its most potent and horrifying symbolic

---

7 See 1 Corinthians 5.13 (but also 2 Corinthians 2.6–8) and Titus 3.10.

8 http://anathema.askdefine.com, accessed 8 April 2014.

expression in the excision of a child's name from the list at the front of the family Bible. As a corollary, this aspect of cursing helps us to see that communion and friendship lie at the heart of what it means to bless, and to be blessed.

Curse in Theology

In considering curses, and how they are overcome, we will think first of all about cursedness in general and about that brokenness of relationship that matters most of all, namely the brokenness of our relation to God. That discussion opens the way for us to think about Christ liberating us from this curse. We can then, within that picture of salvation, think about more particular curses, still pronounced and received today, and about how the Christian might respond. Our resources will come from seeing or setting them within the story of Christ's life, death and resurrection.

We are only three chapters into the book of Genesis, already rich with the language of blessing, when we come across the primordial curses. To the serpent, after the Fall, God says:

Because you have done this,
    cursed are you among all animals
    and among all wild creatures;
upon your belly you shall go,
    and dust you shall eat
    all the days of your life.
I will put enmity between you and the woman,
    and between your offspring and hers;
he will strike your head,
    and you will strike his heel. (Gen. 3.14–15)

And to the woman:

> I will greatly increase your pangs in childbearing;
>> in pain you shall bring forth children,
> yet your desire shall be for your husband,
>> and he shall rule over you. (Gen. 3.16)

And to the man:

> Because you have listened to the voice of your wife,
>> and have eaten of the tree
> about which I commanded you,
>> 'You shall not eat of it',
> cursed is the ground because of you;
>> in toil you shall eat of it all the days of your life;
> thorns and thistles it shall bring forth for you;
>> and you shall eat the plants of the field.
> By the sweat of your face
>> you shall eat bread
> until you return to the ground,
>> for out of it you were taken;
> you are dust,
>> and to dust you shall return. (Gen. 3.17–19)

Already in Genesis we have seen a connection between human beings and the earth: Adam is formed from the dust of the ground and his name itself means something like 'earthling', derived from the Hebrew word for earth or ground. By a happy coincidence, our word 'human' has much the same derivation, although it belongs within a different language group from the Hebrew. It shares the same root as *humus* or earth. Eve's name is also significant, deriving from the Hebrew for life, since she is 'the mother of all living [human beings]' (Gen. 3.20).

These links between humanity, life and the earth form the backdrop for those curses, which relate to both the ground and labour, in both senses of that word: work and childbirth. Materiality and all it means is central here but we should notice that earthiness, and materiality, is not the problem. The message here is not that these things are bad in themselves. Precisely because they are good they can be made less good; because they are *good* they can be cursed.

The rebellion of our putative first parents, in the story, is a rebellion against this vocation to be creatures, to be earthlings. They rejected that vocation and sought to go beyond their nature and their earthiness, wanting to 'be like God' (Gen. 3.5).[9] The resulting curse is worked out in terms of how their vocation has previously been defined: in labour of both sorts,[10] and in a new stubbornness on the part of the earth. Augustine diagnosed the root of sin as pride and described it as 'a perverse desire for height'. There is therefore, again, something fitting to the horizontality of the curse, seen in the face of the earth that is tilled and in the snake going upon its belly.[11]

At this point we might ask whether *God* curses the human race here, and the whole earth, as an active intervention. Theologians have said so but they have also recognized that there is a sense of 'payback' woven into the very nature of wrongdoing, which God does not need to 'impose' from the outside. In that sense we *curse ourselves* by the waywardness

---

9 We will return to the link between a very general sense of 'curse' and living outside of one's nature and vocation below (pp. 113–18).

10 We might want to broaden our sense of human vocation today, beyond men working the ground and women bearing children – not least because it is women who also work on the land in many cultures.

11 We can also note that one common word for cursing (*qâlal*) has the sense of 'being small or contemptible' – Joseph Auneau, 'Blessing – A Biblical Theology', in Jean-Yves Lacoste (ed.), *Encyclopedia of Christian Theology* (London: Routledge, 2004), p. 218.

and foolishness of our actions. Augustine of Hippo makes this point about sin in general, and its consequences, in commenting on Psalm 7.14–16:

> When God punishes sinners, He does not inflict His evil on them, but leaves them to their own evil. 'Behold', saith the Psalmist, 'he hath been in labour with injustice, he hath conceived toil; brought forth iniquity. He hath opened a pit and dug it: and he is fallen into the hole he made. His sorrow shall be turned on his own head: and his iniquity shall come down upon his crown.' When therefore God punishes, He punishes as a judge those that transgress the law, not by bringing evil upon them from Himself, but by driving them on to that which they have chosen, to fill up the sum of their misery.[12]

Even at this point in Genesis, however, even in this pronouncement of the curse under which all of creation languishes because of disobedience, curse does not have the final word – or not, at least, according to the traditional interpretation of the Church. Since early days this passage has been seen as containing the first intimation of the gospel. On that account it has been called the *protoevangelium*, meaning the 'first Gospel'. The significant phrase is 'I will put enmity between you [the serpent] and the woman, and between your offspring and hers; he will strike your head, and you will strike his heel' (Gen. 3.15). All of humanity is that 'offspring', since Eve is the 'mother of all living', but the truest and representative human being, in whom all human

---

12 *Enarrationes in Psalmos*, V.10. Translation from Augustine, in *An Augustine Synthesis*, ed. Erich Przywara (London: Sheed & Ward, 1945).

destiny is invested, is Christ.[13] He is the second Adam, born of the second Eve (as the early Christian Fathers soon came to call Mary), whose obedience contrasted with Eve's disobedience and opened the way for this titanic struggle: that 'enmity', taken to its further pitch of intensity. That strife saw the serpent's head crushed but, since it was achieved by the cross, Christ does not overcome the serpent without himself being wounded, even – indeed – upon his heel.

The sense of strife here indicates that salvation is not some notional thing, merely a change of the way affairs are regarded by God, but something achieved in the world. This note of activity and striving suggests that we are not bound to face the conditions of the curse in a mood of dejected passivity – quietism, as it is sometimes called. While we are under a curse that bears upon labour we need not acquiesce in its effects. Decent labour laws are a good thing, as also is adequate – even excellent – obstetrics. A large proportion of the world's population lacks either.

Theological Angles on Undoing the Curse

From the curse, Christ redeems us. When it comes to asking how that redemption works, some Christians will want to work out a mechanism in detail while others will not. Theories of 'penal substitution', for instance, can easily be adapted to work with curses: God does the cursing and God is able to curse someone else instead, in order to spare us. Readers are likely to find that satisfying, or not, in the same measure as they find accounts of the atonement

---

13 Paul makes a parallel point in relation to Christ as the offspring of Abraham: 'Now the promises were made to Abraham and to his offspring; it does not say, "And to offsprings", as of many; but it says, "And to your offspring", that is, to one person, who is Christ' (Gal. 3.16).

satisfying that are cast in terms of the transfer of punishment from the guilty to the innocent. As an alternative account, rescue from the curse might be spelt out in parallel to what are often called 'ransom' or 'victory' theories of the atonement: we are under the devil's curse but we are delivered out of his power either by the payment of a price or through a victory by which he forfeits his claim. These images were clearly part of the Christian tradition from the beginning, but we might be committing a fundamental mistake – a mistake of genre or category – by supposing that in any such discussion we are explicating a logical mechanism. That observation calls for some comments about method when it comes to thinking about theology, and about the atonement in particular.

The first half of this book considers some of the principal doctrines of the Church in terms of how they relate to the topic of blessing. Reaching the atonement, we might remember that this is one of the few areas of the faith where precise definitions are largely missing. When it comes to the question of Christ's humanity and divinity or to the doctrine of the Trinity, we have definitive teachings, worked out in the early days of the Church: in Christ two natures are united in one Person; in the Trinity three Persons share one nature. Nothing like that surfaced when it came to the atonement. The Church has not seen fit to say that this and not that formulation stands as the only correct way to understand how we are redeemed by the life, death and resurrection of Jesus. We can think of a number of good reasons of this. For one thing, definitions were often provided only in the face of disputes and in response to positions that seemed to be positively unhelpful – positions that we call heresies. Such disputes and wrong turns mark the history of thought about Christ and about God. The same cannot be said about discussion of redemption. It was what everyone took for granted – that Jesus is the saviour of the world – whatever else they might have disagreed about.

Moreover, the New Testament itself simply has too much to say about redemption for us to be able to make a later hard and fast codification. The New Testament authors present the saving work of Christ to us by means of many images and metaphors: Christ ransoms us; he defeats sin and death; he is sacrificed for us; he is the shepherd who has come to guide us, for instance.[14] Later theologians could not, without denying the biblical witness, suggest that one approach, and only one, was valid when it came to understanding salvation.

We can therefore approach the atonement in many ways, as if this act of God – involving as it does his coming in flesh, his death and resurrection – is simply too extraordinary for us even to begin to comprehend if we view it from only one angle. Christians of different traditions can legitimately place a different emphasis on different viewpoints but they should not go so far as to deny a place for any of them in their theology, prayer and praise. Among those vistas onto the atonement we can find ones grounded in ideas of blessing and of curse. They are not perhaps particularly prominent in contemporary discussions. It will suit our purpose, however, in this book, to turn to the accounts that do relate to blessing and curse, to see what light those themes throw on the atonement and to see what the atonement teaches us about blessing and curse.

The central passage of Scripture when it comes to a curse-and-blessing approach to the atonement is in Galatians: 'Christ redeemed us from the curse of the law by becoming

14 For instance, Matthew 20.28; 1 Timothy 2.6; 1 Corinthians 5.7; Ephesians 5.2; John 10.1–16; Hebrews 13.20.

a curse for us – for it is written, "Cursed is everyone who hangs on a tree"' (Gal. 3.13). Here Paul is quoting a rather obscure part of the law concerning capital punishment:

> When someone is convicted of a crime punishable by death and is executed, and you hang him on a tree, his corpse must not remain all night upon the tree; you shall bury him that same day, for anyone hung on a tree is under God's curse. You must not defile the land that the LORD your God is giving you for possession. (Deut. 21.22–23)

There is something so horrible, for the Hebrew mind, about being 'hung upon a tree' that the wrongdoer must not be exposed that way too long or – for reasons we might not fully appreciate – the whole land will be defiled. Whatever is going on in that passage, it leaves us with the principle that is taken up by Paul in Galatians: 'Cursed is everyone who hangs on a tree.' In the crucifixion Christ entered into cursedness (of which hanging on a tree is a paradigmatic example), even into the depths of cursedness. We can appreciate this quite directly by seeing how much the act of crucifixion embodies the human cursed condition, first in terms of death – and a terrible death at that – and second because human beings are cursed in performing such acts, indeed even in being able to conceive of such an act.

We might be familiar with accounts of the atonement that see Christ as facing down sin, evil or death. With Galatians 3 in mind we can also say that Jesus faced down our cursedness. Apart from the link that comes through the reference to Deuteronomy, we can see other aspects of cursedness to the crucifixion. For one thing, curses are about exclusion, and Christ was crucified outside the city walls, near the rubbish dump (John 19.20). This is part of his taking on the exclusion from life and abundance of his people. Furthermore curse is associated with defilement. Crucifixion is a profoundly degrading form of execution, with the derision of the crowd standing as part of that (Mark 15.28–32; Matt. 27.39–44; Luke 23.35–39). It was further compounded for the Jewish mind – and not only the Jewish mind – with the place of Christ's crucifixion being one of death and dead bodies, which is one interpretation of what it means for Golgotha to be called 'the place of the skull' (because of the remains of those previously executed or because the site was near a graveyard). There is no reason to suppose that Joseph of Arimathea's nearby tomb was an isolated example.[15] If we associate blessing with prosperity and life, then upon the cross Christ endured the opposite: not only in that he faced death and that he died but also that he was beaten, stripped of his clothing, thirsty and isolated.

As to how this 'works', how it is that Christ's entering into human cursedness redeems us, an analytic answer may not be forthcoming. Indeed, it might be a mistake to seek such an analytic 'answer', as I have already suggested. The closest approach we have to the logic at work here is the logic of poetry and of praise. It is a hymnic logic – one of wonder. The all-blessed one took upon himself the position of being cursed, and his blessedness overcame cursedness. This is more to be proclaimed and praised than worked out in analytic detail. To ask for a mechanism is not to ask for too much but for too little, as if redemption could be compressed to the parsimonious logic of necessity: because of x, y necessarily followed. In contrast, the logic of redemption is one of excess. Part of what that means

---

15 See 'Mount Calvary', in *The Catholic Encyclopedia*, www.catholic. org/encyclopedia/view.php?id=2412, accessed 10 April 2014.

is that we need not build our entire doctrine of salvation on this retrieval-of-curse approach or upon any other one approach for that matter. Overcoming the curse is one of a patchwork of overlapping accounts of the atonement.

Blessing and Cursing in Culture

The business of cursing and being cursed as a contemporary human activity does not figure equally in all cultures. In all probability it comes to feature less prominently in any culture around the world as it tends towards the global category that we call 'development'. Or at least it is most likely to feature less prominently in an explicitly acknowledged way. For one thing, as such 'development' takes hold we interact with one another in less and less meaningful ways, and our awareness of a metaphysical dimension to life is attenuated. On account of that, explicit cursing is less likely to feature overtly on the map of even occasional human experience. All scare quotes aside, the eclipse of explicit cursing is clearly a good thing, on its own terms, although we might think that our current state in the West – if it involves loss of meaningful interaction and of metaphysical awareness – is itself a sort of curse.

All this said, a sense of living under a curse will feature as something pastorally significant in the lives of some readers. Sometimes this will be experienced as direct curse, a supernatural invocation with occult associations. Sometimes it will belong to a broader category of deliberately expressed ill will or a desire for misfortune invoked upon another. That is also a form of curse, not least because it is invoked against categories that are central to blessing, such as life and prosperity. These dispositions and intentions may be expressed with phrases such as 'Damn you', which is perhaps rarely used today with its full theological freight, or with statements that deny forgiveness: 'Take it to your grave' or something similar. An even more diffuse set of beliefs, proximate to curses but clearly not in entirely the same class, is the sense of having come into 'bad luck'. The cultural resonances will be different in different places. In the UK it might be associated with Friday the thirteenth or walking under a ladder.

A variety of angles suggest themselves as part of a theological and practical reply to curses. A pastor, in particular, might choose among them as a medic might rummage about in a doctor's bag. The challenge is to find the response that best communicates the blessing and hope offered by Christ to a particular person in a particular situation.

A significant but not exhaustive aspect of a Christian reply will involve exposing the situation to the light of reason. This is not an invitation to be dismissive of anyone's worries or of the spiritual aspect of life. It might, however, be an invitation to live with the 'renewed mind' that Paul prized so highly (Rom. 12.2). The Christian faith treats human reason as a thing of dignity, not least because reason is part of the image of the Triune God within us, the Second Person being called *Logos* – 'Word' or 'reason'. In the prologue to John's Gospel, where the idea of the *Logos* is introduced and discussed, the Word is linked to light: 'in him was life, and the life was the light of all people' (John 1.4). God's truth, revealed to us not only *in* Christ but *as* Christ, pours light on a situation. 'The light shines in the darkness', the Gospel continues 'and the darkness did not overcome it' (John 1.6). Part of this 'darkness', which is to be overcome by the light of Christ, is the darkness of ignorance and superstition. We come across that theme in the New Testament Epistles, for instance in Colossians, where we are warned: 'See to it that no one takes you captive through philosophy and empty deceit, according to human tradition, according to the elemental spirits of the universe, and not according to Christ' (Col. 2.8).

One element of the Christian response to cursing, therefore, is to resort to a healthy dose of reason. That need not be seen, and should not, as some hollow desacralization of the world. We are simply being realistic, particularly about the flimsier sort of worries that might come our way. Fear about the date of a particular Friday, or about having walked under a ladder, can and should be met with a sensibly robust attitude about their real power or lack of it, or of a black cat for that matter, or of crossing one's fingers. This is not rationalism; it is a dimension of Christian freedom, which is another quiet but significant emphasis of the Epistles. Consider, for example, 'For freedom Christ has set us free. Stand firm, therefore, and do not submit again to a yoke of slavery' (Gal. 5.1) or 'Now the Lord is the Spirit, and where the Spirit of the Lord is, there is freedom' (2 Cor. 3.17).

This profound sense that the Christian is called to freedom and inherits freedom at baptism is a good general basis for responding to the other sorts of cursing mentioned above: the explicit curse, the declaration of ill will or malicious hopes or a brooding sense of enmity or unforgiveness. Freedom here rests not on some magical removal of a curse but on inhabiting the freedom that is found in Christ, 'if the Son makes you free, you will be free indeed' (John 8.36), and of living under his Lordship: 'the one who is in you is greater than the one who is in the world' (1 John 4.4).

Where a sense of curse has arisen in a relationship, perhaps with a friend or member of one's family (since when such things happen, they usually happen between people who are close, not between those who hardly know one another), a good response is to seek for such reconciliation as can be achieved. Here again we would be following Paul's advice: 'If it is possible, so far as it depends on you, live peaceably with all' (Rom. 12.18). Reaching out in this way is a proper response, both because reconciliation is good on its own terms and because it means that we have 'done our best'. It also conforms to the general Christian principle of meeting a curse with a blessing, as far as we are able. We find that advice in the same chapter of Romans: 'Bless those who persecute you; bless and do not curse them' (Rom. 12.14).[16] Practically speaking this may involve making an expression of good will in reply to an expression of ill will, or it might involve an expression of forgiveness in reply to a 'retention' of sins (where the fault is fairly obviously mutual – we try to forgive, even if they do not), or an expression of regret and request for forgiveness (where the fault lies fairly unambiguously on our side).[17] If we seek forgiveness and it is withheld, even after an expression of remorse, the best course may be to seek the forgiveness of God as mediated in objective terms – helpfully objective terms – through the ministry of the Church, through the sacrament that is variously called 'confession', 'penance' or 'the sacrament of reconciliation'.[18] Nor should the Church's response to fear, confusion or guilt be seen as in conflict with what God provides through human wisdom and compassion. If a perception of being cursed might be associated with some element of mental ill health, then part

---

16 As also, for instance, in Luke 6.28; 1 Corinthians 4.12; 1 Peter 3.9.

17 I have discussed this in relation to preparedness for the end of life in Sioned Evans and Andrew Davison, *Care for the Dying: A Practical and Pastoral Guide* (London: Canterbury Press, 2014), pp. 104–7.

18 On this, see my *Why Sacraments?* (London: SPCK/Eugene, OR: Wipf & Stock, 2013), pp. 129–41.

of a Christian response is also to suggest that the person concerned receive the best support that is available from experts in that field.

Where there has been significant hurt we should not be glib about how difficult forgiveness and reconciliation can be. Sometimes the nearest we can come to forgiving someone completely is wanting to be able to forgive him or her, or to want to wish well for someone, rather than actually being able to express that wish. This is a good first step, as is the decision to commend the situation to God, to be redeemed as he sees fit – for both them and us – in his good time.

We have touched upon one resource of the Church, which is the sacrament of reconciliation. The objectivity of sacramental grace can be enormously useful as part of a response to a sense of cursedness, and that obviously takes in the two greatest sacraments as well: baptism and the Eucharist. The message of baptism is one of freedom – a freedom accomplished through dying with Christ and rising again with him. This is a central theme for Paul when it comes to freedom: the dead have a particularly pronounced form of freedom, and we have died with Christ (Rom. 6.5–11). Christians in previous ages – and in other places today – who took or take the spiritual battle more seriously than many do in contemporary Europe, at least, looked back to baptism as the definitive source of freedom from evil and evil powers. This is expressed to this day in the Easter liturgy, where the resurrection of Christ and our baptism participation in that is seen as crossing the Red Sea: just as the waters closed in and drowned the Egyptians, so the waters of baptism drown anything that has a hold on us. Part, then, of the Christian response to curses and cursing is to stand confidently in what has been achieved for us in baptism. Perhaps the most important element of teaching needed here is to underline that baptism is not something that happened in the past, something done, over and, in that sense, 'used up'. The effect of baptism – its 'grace', as theologians put it – is as fresh today as it was the day we received the sacrament.[19] If a pastor is meeting a sense of curse with a set of prayers or some liturgical form, then sprinkling with holy water – which is principally a symbol of the water of baptism – may be a useful element, for this reason.

Alongside baptism we should also consider the Eucharist. Down the centuries this part of communal Christian life has been seen as the summit of Christian prayer and encounter with Christ. Although different traditions of Christianity might disagree with each other as to precisely what is happening at the Eucharist, they are unlikely to disagree that the Eucharist is the principal moment in the Church's regular cycle of life where we are brought into the presence of Christ and into contact with the Easter mystery of his death and resurrection. Here we encounter Christ, who was cursed for us, who took all spiritual misfortune and enmity upon himself and who rose victorious; here we encounter the fullness of the love of God and, as we read in 1 John: 'There is no fear in love, but perfect love casts out fear; for fear has to do with punishment, and whoever fears has not reached perfection in love' (1 John 4.18). Priests in some traditions will be accustomed to 'offering a Eucharist' or 'offering a Mass' as a prayer for a particular hope or desire (often called an 'intention' in this context). However we do it and however we understand it, bringing a situation that bears a sense of cursedness before God through the Eucharist, in union with Christ's offering upon the cross

---

19 I have written about this in *Why Sacraments?*, p. 29.

and his resurrection, is about the most significant response the Church can make.

In certain extreme cases the priest might also want to pronounce an end to a curse (particularly one that has been invoked with parallel solemnity), not least by meeting it with a blessing. On this score we might note that blessings have been seen to bear an element of protection from evil and evil powers for a significant stretch of Christian history.[20] The association of blessing with protection is likely to go far back into pre-history. Scholars of blessing observe particular attention to this element with the advent of a set of prayer books called the Frankish-Gelasian sacramentaries (eighth century).[21] Prayers for protection against evil powers came to new prominence in the eight century as part of the missionary endeavour across Europe. As traditional religions were supplanted, blessings provided a Christian response to a perceived need previously met by pagan religion and magic.[22]

The association of blessings with protection from evil powers remained until the liturgical reforms of the Western Church in the mid-twentieth century. Since then, in contrast, any sense of protection from evil and from the devil has largely been removed. Uwe Lang notes that a typical justification for these changes has been a call for the Church to move away from a 'pessimistic' vision of the world, where evil lurks at the door, to a more optimistic

---

20 Liturgists call this, technically, the 'apotropaic' element of a blessing.

21 Derek A. Rivard, *Blessing the World: Ritual and Lay Piety in Medieval Religion* (Washington, DC: Catholic University of America Press, 2009), p. 32.

22 Pierre-Marie Gy, 'Benedictions', in Joseph R. Strayer (ed.), *Dictionary of the Middle Ages* (New York: Scribner, 1982–9), vol. 2, p. 177. Cited in Rivard, *Blessing the World*, p. 33.

one. Lang goes on to criticize this shift: 'The theological rationale for this [development] claims to be biblical, but would appear to be oblivious of the fact that Christ himself, in the Gospel of John, speaks of "the prince of this world" (John 12.31, 14.30, 16.11).'[23] The Lord's Prayer, after all, contains the petition 'deliver us from evil [*or* the evil one]' (Matt. 6.13).

We should, certainly, recognize the goodness of creation and insist that it remains a place where we can encounter God, despite the fallenness of things. However, not also to see that the world needs redemption, and that human life is fragile before the all too real forces arrayed against it, reveals the glibness of late twentieth-century optimism. In this way, many Western liturgies of blessing today simply fail to take redemption sufficiently seriously, or the reality of evil and suffering, or the fear in which people often live.

The Evil Eye and an Evil Tongue

We can let ourselves off the hook too easily when it comes to cursing. Very few of us curse people directly, even occasionally. That is all to the good. The scriptural writers, however, point to some allied activities and attitudes, which, if they are not exactly curses, are in adjoining territory. These remain prevalent today. I have in mind ways of perceiving and of speaking, which the Scriptures associate with the eye and with the tongue.

When it comes to the eye we might take our lead from the parable of the Labourers in the Vineyard (Matt. 20.1–16). They are called by the master from the recruiting yard of

---

23 Uwe Michael Lang, 'Theologies of Blessing: Origins and Characteristics of *De benedictionibus* (1984)', *Antiphon* 15.1 (2011), p. 44.

the town square at various hours of the day, from early in the morning until close to the end of the working day. In contrast to what any of the workers were expecting, at the end of the day the owner instructs his steward to pay everyone the same amount: the 'penny' or denarius that he had agreed with those who had worked for the whole day, and which represented the average workman's average daily wage. Jesus introduced the parable by saying that 'the kingdom of heaven is like a landowner' (Matt. 20.1) who hires workers. In other words, if we want to know what the kingdom of heaven is like, it is like this. The point is about the generosity of God, which theologians call grace.

There is a sort of abundance to the handing out of wages, which seems aligned to blessing. This generosity, however, is not received well by all. Those who had laboured longest begrudge his generosity (Matt. 20.11). This reaction is directly comparable to the older son in the parable of the Prodigal Son (Luke 15.28–30). The Greek is rather unusual and the Authorized Version is more literal than most recent translations: not 'are you envious because I am generous?' (NRSV) but 'Is thine eye evil, because I am good?' (Matt. 20.15).

We might think that the 'evil eye' is an Italian or Islamic superstition, but the phrase is found in both the Old and New Testaments.[24] An evil eye is one that looks enviously, meanly, begrudgingly. This is reflected in the etymology of the Latin word for envy, which is *invidia*. Literally it means 'to look upon maliciously', coming from *in-* (meaning 'upon') and *videre* (meaning 'to see'). Envy is one of the

---

24 See, for instance, Mark 7.22, where it is often translated as 'envy' or in the AV as 'an evil eye'. For a treatment of this idea in the Old Testament and in the writings of the rabbis, see Rivka Ulmer, *The Evil Eye in the Bible and in Rabbinic Literature* (Hoboken, NJ: KTAV Publishing House, 1994).

'deadly sins', and of all the deadly sins, envy is the mean-est and most unproductive. As Augustine put it, envy is 'hatred of another's happiness';[25] Frederic Harton called it 'discontent with others' good'.[26] Envy is greed with the good bits taken out: at least a greedy person desires real goods, even if they are minor ones and sought immoder-ately. The greedy person might pass over greater goods for the sake of lesser ones, but at least he rejoices in the good-ness of the thing desired. In contrast, envy fails to rejoice in the good but wants to destroy it so that other people cannot have it. The meanness of envy was magnificently put by Gore Vidal in a phrase that should make our blood run cold: 'whenever a friend succeeds, a little something in me dies'.[27]

We might not live, in the West, in a world full of explicit curses, but we do live in a world full of envy. We might usefully see an 'evil eye' as a sort of curse, not least because it reacts negatively to the good provision, or blessing, of another. Envy is a contravention of Paul's injunction to 'Rejoice with those who rejoice, weep with those who weep' (Rom. 12.15). To rid ourselves of this 'curse' – and its associated tendency towards ratcheting up the general cursedness of the world – the task is all about seeing, as the 'evil eye' metaphor helps us to appreciate. The task is to look upon others and see their suffering as my suffer-ing and their gain as my own. The best way to train our eyes to see without envy is to take the grace of God as our interpretative key in all that we see or consider: others' existence is a gift, as is mine; their life and all that is needed

25 Augustine, *The Literal Meaning of Genesis*, trans. John Hammond Taylor (New York: Newman Press, 1982), book 11, Chapter 14.

26 F. P. Harton, *The Elements of the Spiritual Life: A Study in Ascetical Theology* (London: SPCK, 1932), p. 141.

27 *Sunday Times Magazine*, 16 September 1973.

for life is a gift, and so is mine – and their life and their flourishing is a gift also to me.

We might also notice that envy can only take root if there is a prior sense of dissociation and isolation. We can only be envious if we think that our good is one thing and our neighbour's good is another. This has become a profoundly well-entrenched perspective, ever since the early days of modernity. We see it, for instance, in the definition of Thomas Hobbes – truly horrific in its way – that the basic state of play for the human community is 'the war of all against all'.[28] Accept *that* as a basic assumption about the world, and envy will arise quite naturally. The Christian reply is not simply to say that envy is a bad thing; it is also to criticize the assumptions upon which it rests, since my good and my neighbour's good are not in competition. I can be happy that you are happy and, since my best good lies in the common good, whatever I can do to help you, helps me also.

From the eye we can move on to the tongue. The etymology of the word blessing – in 'speaking well' – has already proved instructive. Not everything we would want to say about the business of blessing is to found there, but much is. From that we might guess that particular attention should be paid to speech when it comes to how Christians might embody blessing in the world. What we do and do not say, and how we say it, are likely to be significant. That observation, by negation, then also points to the significance of everyday speech as a source of cursedness, even if we rarely form sentences that involve the verb 'to curse'.

---

28 This phrase occurs in the preface of his *De Cive* (1642) as *bellum omnium contra omnes*. Similar phrases occur in his English words, such as the 'warre of every one against every one' (*Leviathan*, Chapter 14).

Speech receives considerable attention in the Scriptures, not least in the Wisdom literature. The book of Proverbs goes so far as to say that 'Death and life are in the power of the tongue' (Prov. 18.21). Turning to the New Testament, we have Christ's comment that 'it is not what goes into the mouth that defiles a person, but it is what comes out of the mouth that defiles' (Matt. 15.11), since it is 'out of the abundance of the heart [that] the mouth speaks' (Matt. 12.34). The Epistle of James is another, particularly rich, repository of reflections upon the vices of the tongue, especially in the discussion of corrupt and corrupting speech in chapter three. This is introduced with the comment that 'all of us make many mistakes. Anyone who makes no mistakes in speaking is perfect, able to keep the whole body in check with a bridle' (James 3.2). At the end of this discussion we come across an explicit mention of blessing and cursing:

> With it we bless the Lord and Father, and with it we curse those who are made in the likeness of God. From the same mouth come blessing and cursing. My brothers and sisters, this ought not to be so. Does a spring pour forth from the same opening both fresh and brackish water? Can a fig tree, my brothers and sisters, yield olives, or a grapevine figs? No more can salt water yield fresh. (James 3.9–12)

If we are to bless God, then we should not curse human beings, and in as much as blessing broadens out to 'speaking well of', then 'cursing' here broadens out to include speaking ill of someone. That theme is found elsewhere in the New Testament. We find particular attention to the good that our words can do – and even more to the evil – in Ephesians and Colossians: 'Let no evil talk come out of your mouths, but only what is useful for building up, as there is need, so that your words may give grace to those who hear' (Eph. 4.29) and 'Let your speech always be gracious, seasoned with salt, so that you may know how you ought to answer everyone' (Col. 4.6). In every age, 'bridling the tongue' is a principal component of Christian discipleship and one, as we have seen, closely associated with both blessing and curse.

Cursing and curses cannot be allowed to capture too much of our attention in this book, but they are part of any presentation of blessing that hopes to be even half comprehensive. The Church, the pastor and the theologian have many resources with which to address curses. Responding to explicit curses, however, is not the whole picture, just as refraining from cursing people explicitly is not the whole part of Christian self-discipline in this area. We have considered some of the ways in which how we speak in everyday life, and how we perceive the world and respond to the flourishing of others belong within the remit of blessing and cursing. Living as a blessing and not as a curse, it seems, calls for some fairly radical, countercultural growth in holiness.

6

Blessing and Salvation in Ministry and Mission

Blessing occupies a contested place in the Church and in Christian theology. Sometimes the subject has met benign neglect; at other times blessing has aroused outright hostility or at least suspicion. To see why, we can turn to the classic twentieth-century discussion of blessing from a theological perspective, Claus Westermann's *Blessing in the Bible and the Life of the Church*. Westermann noted just how much theologians have tended to approach blessing as if it stood in opposition to a focus on redemption, either in theology or in the life of the Church.[1]

The purpose of this chapter is to deny that redemption and blessing are fundamentally in tension. In doing that we will consider a parallel tendency, common today, to oppose mission and ministry. We should not, however, arrive at a position of amity and peace too hastily, since a sense of conflict between blessing and redemption, and certainly that sense of a disjunction between ministry and mission,

---

1 Claus Westermann, *Blessing in the Bible and the Life of the Church* (Philadelphia, PA: Fortress Press, 1978; first published in German in 1968). That contrast would be stronger within Westermann's own German Protestant tradition than it would be, for instance, in the Roman Catholic Church.

is endemic in today's Church (and especially in my own), even if it is not always cast explicitly in those terms.[2]

As an example we might consider the extent to which contemporary Christianity has segregated into varieties concerned primarily with celebration and others primarily concerned with judgement, with a corresponding emphasis either on this world or the world to come. 'Ministry', in this polarized and rather two-dimensional account, is concerned with the joys and trials of this life and cements embeddedness in this world and its patterns. We can see the links to blessing here. In contrast, those who reject 'old models' based on 'ministry' often do so in the name of mission and reject just such a 'blessing' element (although it is not necessarily given that name). They want the Church to preach repentance, not blessing, and urge us to think not about this world but about the world to come.

Preaching Blessing without Redemption

This dichotomy serves neither ministry nor mission particularly well. All the same, there are those who subscribe to one extreme or the other. As an example of someone who takes blessing to an unhealthy extreme, consciously opposing redemption in the process, we might consider the Dutch theologian Reit Bons-Storm.[3] Arguing in feminist terms, she turned to blessing as a way to overcome the

---

2 If this book provides something of a perspective on systematic theology, worked out in terms of blessing, then this chapter could be said to be concerned with ecclesiology, eschatology and their relation.

3 Reit Bons-Storm, 'Beyond the Obsession with Guilt and Atonement: Towards a Theology of Blessing and Its Implications for Our Practices', in Wilhelm Gräb and Lars Charbonnier (eds), *Secularization Theories, Religious Identity and Practical Theology: Developing International Practical Theology for the 21st Century* (Berlin: Lit, 2009), p. 77.

language of redemption. For her, talk of salvation, sin and sacrifice are irredeemably flawed. Fortunately, her approach is unusual.

Bons-Storm's research in the Netherlands showed the presence of considerable residual faith among people who believe in God but who do not attend church (and for whom the death of Jesus is 'not all-important'). She suggests a model of mission that is not based on the traditional proclamation of salvation, but rather on the message of 'an unconditionally loving God', who is 'with people' in their daily lives and gives them 'strength and courage' in the midst of difficulties. Pastoral care, on this view, becomes 'an affirmation of this [still instinctive] trust in God's presence in their lives'. She calls this affirmation 'blessing' and recommends 'a theory and a practice of pastoral work . . . not based on the paradigm of sin, cross, redemption, but on the God who blesses'.[4]

Bons-Storm's proposals are based on all sorts of false oppositions and they do not take sufficiently seriously the degree to which a decisive confrontation with sin and evil is part of the good news. Despite all the problems, however, her suggestions can be useful as a provocation. They remind us that we have every reason to reject the 'secularization thesis' – the assumption that adherence to religion, and its significance in public and daily life, are in inevitable decline. The talk today among academic sociologists of religion is that our times belong to 'post-secularity'.[5] In that case, churches need to find ways to connect the message of the Church and the practices of the Christian

---

4 Bons-Storm, 'Beyond the Obsession', p. 79.

5 A good example is the retraction, by the editor of *The Economist* (John Micklethwait) and its Washington bureau chief (Adrian Wooldridge), of the idea that religion was on the wane in *God is Back: How the Global Rise of Faith is Changing the World* (London: Penguin, 2010).

community with the sort of real residual religious beliefs and sentiments Bons-Storm discussed. Blessing allows us to make links between people in their everyday lives and the God whom the Church proclaims. As we shall see, far from this being in contrast to the message of redemption, the practice of blessing can provide an opening for that message and can be part of the way it takes hold.

A Proper Place for Redemption – and for Blessing

We have identified two opposed tendencies, which we can present as parodies although they are nonetheless encountered within the Church: blessing-without-redemption and redemption-without-blessing, which we might also call celebrating-without-purifying and purifying-without-celebrating. We have, on the one hand, a desire to leave things as they are and, on the other, an assumption that God rubs things out and starts again.

Those who want to uphold redemption have an important point, and not least against a too accepting warmth towards the current state of things. Throughout the New Testament we find attention to the saving work of God, which involves being saved 'from' the world (for example, John 15.19 or Gal. 1.4). We might think of words from 1 Peter: 'Beloved, I urge you as aliens and exiles to abstain from the desires of the flesh that wage war against the soul' (1 Pet. 2.11), or we might think of the heroes of the faith discussed in Hebrews 11, who 'confessed that they were strangers and foreigners on the earth . . . seeking a homeland . . . Therefore God is not ashamed to be called their God; indeed, he has prepared a city for them' (Heb. 11.13–14, 16).

The Church and the Christian are called to be something radically different from the world around them: 'be blameless and innocent, children of God without blemish in the midst of a crooked and perverse generation, in which you shine like stars in the world' (Phil. 2.14–15). However, any such witness, otherworldly in a sense though it may be, is at the same time for the sake of the world. In the words of the Epistle of James, we are redeemed, or reborn, 'so that we would become a kind of first fruits of his creatures' (James 1.18). On that logic, any difference or separation from the world is not to be rejoiced in for its own sake, as if it were the desired end. Our redemption, wonderful though it is on its own terms, should also always be seen as being for the sake of the redemption of others.

In any case, these descriptions of being set apart – like strangers and pilgrims, like stars in the world, like a kind of first fruits – are clearly not at variance with the idea of blessing, which is itself concerned *with setting apart*. Blessing involves dedication, and is a part in God's process of making things holy. Nor need the theology and practice of blessing be caught off guard by a proper concern for the life of the world to come. Part of what it means to bless someone – or something or somewhere – is to point out how life now relates to the life of the world to come, and to God as the final destiny of all things. When we bless something we confess that it belongs to God, not least because it comes from God and finds its proper consummation in him. The business of blessing is therefore not only a matter of acknowledging that things come from God but also a recognition that everything that comes under the shadow of God's grace – and who can say how wide that shadow might be – is being drawn to God as the one in whom it will find its eternal fulfilment. We are often forgetful of this orientation; indeed, we are even usually and chronically forgetful. Blessing is an act that helps us to remember and to realign our imagination, collectively as well as individually.

We should admit that, with blessing, we walk something of a tightrope in relation of the life of the world to come. On the one hand we should not act as if the kingdom has already come in all its fullness but, on the other, neither can we defer every aspect of that kingdom to a coming world, sealed off from this one. Such a division, we should remember, is particularly convenient for the unjust oppressors of this world. Instead, we pray, and look, for the coming of the kingdom while also celebrating and working for whatever anticipations and 'first fruits' might be possible.

Blessing, therefore, need not be an uncritical endorsement of the world as we find it; nor need it be an evasion of the properly apocalyptic note we read in Paul, in the Gospels and elsewhere. For all blessing celebrates and hallows what we find in the world, the Christian approach does so in a way – simply by being properly and theologically Christian – that includes a note of rupture from the patterns of a fallen order, and of the irruption of the coming kingdom. Blessing, here, bears political freight. We see this, for instance, in singling out for blessing all that constitutes the basic and simple means for life – a home, food and so on – rather than luxuries, which are *less* worthy of blessing. Homes receive the dignity of being blessed; large plasma televisions do not. Or consider how far we are from a comfortable endorsement of the status quo when we bless someone taking up a role that is of great benefit for the Church and the community but is not going to earn anyone a great deal of money. We bless the beginning of the ministry of a parish worker; we do not typically bless the beginning of the career of a banker. We also see this dynamic when we refuse to bless any enterprise that stands against the common good. We see it when we bless fields, rivers and seas, so as to confess that provision for what we need for life does not lie in our own hands but in the hands of God and in his 'providence' (which is derived from the same root as 'provide'). This is deeply subversive in a culture that prizes mastery, not least in technological forms.

Lessons to be Learned

Before we become too rosy-eyed about blessing we should return to the idea that there are biblical injunctions to take seriously that are potentially a little uncomfortable for enthusiasts for the subject – injunctions that might be put forward by those who are still suspicious of blessing (or of ministry, for that matter). The message of Jesus burst upon the world in an unsettling way, and aspects of that message certainly warn us against approaching the Christian task as one of 'caretaking'. If blessing belongs to the cycle of the natural order, as it often does, with marriages, births and funerals, then we have also to contend with Christ's injunction to 'Let the dead bury their own dead' (Luke 9.60; Matt. 8.22) and his comment that some are eunuchs 'for the sake of the kingdom of heaven' (Matt. 19.12), or with Paul's argument in favour of celibacy in 1 Corinthians 7. One passage from the chapter in particular bears upon the question in hand:

> brothers and sisters, the appointed time has grown short; from now on, let even those who have wives be as though they had none, and those who mourn as though they were not mourning, and those who rejoice as though they were not rejoicing, and those who buy as though they had no possessions, and those who deal with the world as though they had no dealings with it. For the present form of this world is passing away. (1 Cor. 7.29–31)

We must ask, with all seriousness, whether this renders the business of blessing somehow redundant. Should we limit ourselves, after all, to blessing mission initiatives aimed at recruiting souls for the life of the world to come, and leave it at that? Certainly we have a strong warning that life in the Christian community is not to be worked out as if we had no more than a biological existence.[6] However, we can accept that all this is a valid, even vital, dimension without wishing to abolish blessing or its place in the Christian scheme; rather, these concerns can chasten our understanding of blessing, helping it to be properly Christian. That chastening might be particularly needed, for instance, when blessing is reduced to a get-rich-quick scheme.

Paul's rhetoric in 1 Corinthians is arresting and able to rouse us from complacency. However, the Church has arrived at theological reasons to approve of marriage, comfort the bereaved, and to rejoice joyfully at all that is good. Paul himself gives us every indication that the perspective in this passage needs to be held alongside others, not least in his injunction that we should 'Rejoice with those who rejoice, weep with those who weep' (Rom. 12.15) and his concern that marriage should be honoured (1 Cor. 5).

Our approach to blessing needs to hold a properly apocalyptic dimension alongside other theological principles. We should, for instance, avoid at least two heresies here: not to be Marcionite and write off the Old Testament, with its pattern of blessings, and not to be Gnostic, writing off the material world, the flesh and the family as somehow unworthy of being blessed. For a helpful parallel case, we might turn to the developing tradition of the Church when

---

6 As, of course, we demonstrate by blessing those consecrating themselves to a single life for Christ's sake. The contrast between biological and spiritual existence can be overdone, however, not least since it is often those with a 'spiritual' perspective who also care most about the biological.

it came to burial of the dead. The countercultural injunction to 'Let the dead bury their own dead' did not remain
the dominant principle as the life of the Church progressed.
Indeed, a dignified way of handling dead bodies and a careful and reverent attention to burial became a significant
way in which Christians express much that was important
about their faith within the ancient world and into the present day. Acting in a way that honoured all, irrespective of
background, and that looked for the general resurrection
of the dead, became countercultural in its own way.

Living in Times 'Grown Short'

The wider, historical picture is that the Church was forced
to reinterpret what it meant for 'the appointed time' to
have 'grown short' (1 Cor. 7.29). Paul was clearly writing
from an expectation that the second coming, and the end
of the world, lay just around the corner. As decade followed decade and century followed century, the Church
by no means gave up on that expectation, but Christians
also came to accept that God had a plan for a lengthening
period in which the Church would, necessarily, put down
roots. The situation is parallel to the Babylonian exile,
when the prophet Jeremiah urged the exiles:

> Build houses and live in them; plant gardens and eat what
> they produce. Take wives and have sons and daughters;
> take wives for your sons, and give your daughters in
> marriage, that they may bear sons and daughters; mul-
> tiply there, and do not decrease. But seek the welfare of
> the city where I have sent you into exile, and pray to the
> LORD on its behalf, for in its welfare you will find your
> welfare. (Jer. 29.5–7)

We see this worked out in relation to marriage. Starting with the radical call of Christ, and of Paul for that matter, the early Church looked favourably on celibacy. Indeed, as that tradition grew, some authors went further and began to pour scorn on marriage. That trajectory, thankfully, was not allowed to develop beyond certain bounds, and it soon came under fierce counter-attack from figures such as Augustine of Hippo. However much the celibate vocation was valued (and it could hardly not be valued, given the words of Christ and Paul), thinkers at the centre of gravity of the Church's theological tradition never let those considerations devalue marriage. As they saw it, whether one praised marriage or virginity at any particular moment, it was possible – and proper – to honour each in a way that also honoured the other.[7]

Grace and Nature

Having accepted that the radical call of the gospel can, and should, exercise a chastening influence on anything like a naïve or excessive attention to blessing, we might also ask whether there can be an opposing naïve and excessive tendency that presents the gospel as an otherworldly call of rupture from the present order of the world. One does not need to be entirely committed to following Aquinas in every theological matter to value his maxim that the effect of grace is not to abolish nature but to perfect it.[8] We might remember Christ's saying that he had not come to abolish

---

7 On the contemporary scene, the sort of Christian who might be tempted to favour mission in such a way as to cast it in contradistinction to the blessing of human concerns is not likely to favour a blanket elevation of virginity over marriage for all.

8 *Summa Theologiae* I.1.8 *ad* 2.

the old religious order (the 'law') but to fulfil it (Matt. 5.17) – and there is plenty of blessing in the law. Similarly, the declaration in the book of Revelation that Christ will make 'all things new' (Rev. 21.5) is far more likely – according to the Greek – to mean that he will restore newness to all things than that he will make all things again from scratch, abolishing any connection with what has gone before. The gospel is all about the kingdom of God, and while that kingdom is not simply the same as earthly life as we have known it, neither is it so lacking in structure as to be without opportunities for blessing and all that blessing entails. Jesus said that he had come to bring life and life in all its fullness (John 10.10), and examples from his own life show this did not stand at odds with what human beings down the ages have considered to constitute fullness: he ate and drank (Matt. 11.19; Luke 7.34); he performed his first miracle at a wedding (John 2.1–11); he blessed children (Matt. 19.13; Mark 10.13).

Blessing and Witness

We should deny any intrinsic tension between blessing and redemption, for all they do represent two aspects of the Christian vision that can helpfully complement and criticize one another. As an example of their relation, and how the message of *grace* shines through both, consider, for instance, that blessings are never *sold* within the Church. Christians might take that for granted, but there are other religious traditions and folk traditions of magic where they are. The freedom with which blessings are bestowed itself bears witness to the gratuity of the gospel.

In concluding this chapter we will consider some other ways in which blessing is nothing if it is not part of the mission of the Church, and mission is nothing if it does not come to those who receive it as a blessing. In Chapter 2 we saw that blessing typically has two elements: thanksgiving and invocation – that is to say, an element of acknowledgement of what is good and an element of acknowledgement of what needs to be put right; what Lathrop called *anamnesis* (remembering) and *epiclesis* (calling down). This already demonstrates that an act of blessing is not simply one of celebration; it also bears witness to the need for redemption, and asks for it.

'Invocation', here, might seem most clearly to relate to redemption but remembering (with celebration and thanksgiving) also has much to do with mission.[9] Simply to celebrate creation at all might be countercultural and certainly has been during certain periods of history. Emphasis on the goodness of materiality already puts us beyond the ambit of some of the world's religious traditions down history. To insist, beyond this, that everyone in the world, and all we have – not least our prosperity – are gifts and not of our own independent fabrication is to add insult to injury as far as a certain individualist, libertarian mindset is concerned. We might remember the outrage when President Obama, in the run-up to the 2012 election, claimed that the CEOs of large companies are not the only people responsible for building their success. Whatever we do is a joint exercise: we have only to consider how others have prepared the way for us to be where we stand or how what we do relies on the labour of others. With blessing we shift this claim into a new and heightened register – that God's work is the ultimate precondition for anything we do. This interleaves

9 As, for instance, in the precedent in the Old Testament for linking deliverance with remembrance – and blessing for that matter – at the Passover meal.

with Obama's point: saying that God gives us the good things we enjoy has not usually been separated by theologians from the proposal that God gives us those good things through other people. The offertory prayers in many eucharistic liturgies bear witness to this – that God is the origin of all things and that his gifts are mediated through the work of many ordinary people. The priest takes bread and wine and says, perhaps, something like 'Blessed are you, Lord God of all creation; through your goodness we have this bread to offer, which earth has given, and this wine to offer, the fruit of the vine, both of which human hands have made.'

Blessings, then, articulate various points that belong to the Christian proclamation. Further still, not only do they bear upon its content, they can also be ways to open up opportunities for that proclamation. We might think here not particularly of the sort of blessings typically taken up only by Christians – the blessing of ministries, perhaps, or of a pilgrimage – but rather of those blessings that are performed 'out in the open' or away from the gathered worshipping life of the Church. Those might include the blessing of fields on Rogation Sunday, the blessing of an area with a procession on Corpus Christi, the inaugural blessing of some civic event or monument or the blessing of a house because the occupants – who have rarely been to church – feel disquieted there.

The mission of the Church also takes in the interaction of Christians with members of other religions, and here again blessings are a useful interface. Here we might also consider the relation of the Church to people who adhere to vague non-Christian spiritualities, outside membership of any particular religion.

Many parish priests, especially those concerned to be visible on the streets in an obviously clerical capacity, will witness to the inter-faith potential of a willingness to give a blessing. In my curacy parish a local Hindu family often came to the church to pray. A link had previously been established with them when the clergy stood by them when they were threatened with homelessness: everyone who lives within the parish boundary is a parishioner and might call on the clergy for this sort of support. The family asked for blessings from time to time, for instance when the husband was being admitted to hospital for an operation (on that occasion the laying on of hands seemed appropriate, but not anointing for someone who had not been baptized), or when a child was to travel on a school trip. In their eagerness to be blessed they were more assiduous in seeking God's favour and protection through liturgical means than most Christian members of the parish congregation. The most striking request, one Saturday morning, was for me, as the curate, 'to perform the Church of England's puberty ceremony'. They wanted something equivalent to a Hindu rite to mark the occasion of the daughter's first menstruation. I hope that the service I threw together on the spot, that morning after the daily Eucharist, met the needs of the occasion: some prayers of gathering, the collect for The Birth of the Blessed Virgin Mary,[10] extemporized prayers on the themes of growing up and responsibility presented by the occasion, a Hail Mary before the statue

---

10 'Almighty and everlasting God, who stooped to raise fallen humanity through the child-bearing of blessed Mary: grant that we, who have seen your glory revealed in our human nature and your love made perfect in our weakness, may daily be renewed in your image and conformed to the pattern of your Son Jesus Christ our Lord, who is alive and reigns with you, in the unity of the Holy Spirit, one God, now and for ever' – *Common Worship: Festivals* (London: Church House Publishing, 2008), p. 177.

of the Blessed Virgin and the blessing from the Feast of the Annunciation.

Turning to vaguer outlooks, the idea of blessing has been received with sympathy within the broad but ill-defined range of spiritualities that might be called 'New Age' or 'esoteric' – the sort of approach we find in the 'Mind, Body, Spirit' section of UK bookshops or the 'Metaphysics' section in the USA (to the chagrin of philosophers of metaphysics). That interest in blessing would not merit comment except that it demonstrates a keen continuing fascination with the subject – and a sense of the need for blessing – well beyond the bounds of the Church. This might suggest that the Church is not as 'present' as it might be, offering God's blessing according to Christian forms and practices, and that more diligent and creative blessing could be an open door through which the Church could communicate something of the grace of God and have an opportunity to bear witness to what blessing means within the larger Christian picture. Something more or less parallel was explored by Larry Lenning – although in a thoroughly Muslim context – in his *Blessing in Mosque and Mission*,[11] and as we noted in Chapter 5, the tradition of blessing in the Church seems to have taken on a new character – with more attention given to protection from evil – in the eighth century, as part of a missionary endeavour. The Church wanted to provide all the perceived spiritual benefits of paganism in protection from evil, and more besides (see p. 73).

The approach to take, as I have suggested elsewhere,[12] is to offer what people are inchoately seeking outside the Church and to do so in a way that draws deeply on the

---

11 Larry G. Lenning, *Blessing in Mosque and Mission* (Pasadena, CA: William Carey Library, 1980).

12 Andrew Davison and Alison Milbank, *For the Parish: A Critique of Fresh Expressions* (London: SCM Press, 2010), pp. 108–13.

authentic practices of the Christian faith rather than copying the esoteric rites themselves. We should give people the authentic Christian tradition rather than an attempt on our part to copy their imitation of the Church. A quick search of blessings on web 'alternative spirituality' pages will show just how often those prayers are reworked, paganized versions of Christian texts. Another angle on this world comes from David Spangler's book *Blessing*, where it is clear that the requests he receives to bless things are those commonly associated with a clergyman or -woman in the collective imagination but transferred to a New Age guru.[13]

Blessing, Redemption and Liturgy

A dichotomy between blessing and redemption is a false dichotomy. We see that, for one thing, in the way blessing features in the New Testament Epistles. Almost always the context is one that joins them up to the story of salvation (for example, 2 Cor. 1.3–7; Eph. 1.3–14; 1 Pet. 1.3–9).[14] This bond with redemption is also seen in the default setting

---

13 David Spangler, *Blessing: The Art and the Practice* (New York: Riverhead Books, 2001). Even among New Age teachers, Spangler is unusual for the emphasis he puts on blessing. His book is the distillation of his thought after having run a large number of 'blessing classes'. His presentation of blessing in terms of the manipulation, transfer or sharing of some ill-defined spiritual 'energy' (with only occasional references to 'God' or 'the Source') stands a long way from Christian (or Islamic or Jewish) understandings of blessing, and his suggestion that one might open oneself up to the power and influence of 'non-physical beings' (in the chapter on 'Working with Unseen Forces') aligns the book with sorcery. Nonetheless, it would be churlish not to admit that he offers humane wisdom from time to time.

14 Joseph Auneau, 'Blessing – A Biblical Theology', in Jean-Yves Lacoste (ed.), *Encyclopedia of Christian Theology* (London: Routledge, 2004), p. 219.

for the blessings of the Church, which is a eucharistic one, and the more solemn and all-embracing a blessing might be, the more likely it is to be performed as part of a celebration of Holy Communion. In this way blessing is held in the bosom of that rite which, alongside baptism, most of all recalls the events of our redemption and makes them present to us. In earlier days the blessings of even everyday items – such as food – seems to have been performed during the Eucharist. Today this is retained for the blessing of oils (on Maundy Thursday) and – likely as not – for the consecration of monks and nuns and the blessing of churches. The logic, as Rivard puts it, is 'to highlight the relationship of such blessings to the greatest blessing of all, Christ and his work of redemption'.[15]

With sacraments in mind, we have also seen the bond between blessing and baptism, especially in Chapter 5 on curses and cursing. One of the two most characteristic physical acts associated with blessing is sprinkling with holy water as an invocation of the waters of baptism. The other is making the sign of the cross, the archetypal visual sign of redemption. Remembering these liturgical points, we might return to Westermann's contention, presented at the start of this chapter, that blessing and redemption have been set far apart in his own tradition and even seen as being in antagonism. We could reasonably say in reply that this hang-up belongs within a particularly Protestant approach to church life. If, in contrast, blessings are typically associated with the Eucharist, with baptism (through water) and with the crucifixion (through the sign of the cross), as they typically are in the Catholic West and the

---

15 Derek A. Rivard, *Blessing the World: Ritual and Lay Piety in Medieval Religion* (Washington, DC: Catholic University of America Press, 2009), p. 29.

Orthodox East, then the wedge between blessing and salvation is harder to insert.

It is a perverse disjunction, as Jürgen Moltmann has pointed out in making a helpful point based on usage in his own native language of German, perhaps responding to the same sort of bifurcation that worried Westermann, his compatriot:

> The German word *heiligen* – to make holy, 'to hallow', to sanctify – always has something to do with *heilen*, 'healing'; and so in many languages that show healing has to do with being made whole. In English, holy and whole are closely connected, and not just phonetically. So the sanctification of life includes the healing of life that is sick, and the becoming-whole of a life that has become divided and split.[16]

Blessing occupies both of these registers – hallowing and making whole – and in doing so it bears its own witness that they are not far removed from each other. This is the work of redemption: making whole, healing, sanctifying. It is ultimately to restore us to a state of blessedness and indeed to confer upon us a state of blessedness far beyond anything we could imagine or had before. Blessing and redemption go hand in hand. For the moment there is a proper sense in which they need to balance and complement each other. Perhaps the age between the resurrection and the Second Coming is one of redemption, first of all, but ultimately redemption is for the sake of blessing.

---

16 Jürgen Moltmann, *The Source of Life: The Holy Spirit and the Theology of Life* (London: SCM Press, 1997), p. 52.

7

The Efficacy of Blessings

Writing shortly before his death in 1633, George Herbert had no doubt about the efficacy of blessings:

> Now blessing differs from prayer, in assurance, because it is not performed by way of request, but of confidence, and power, effectually applying God's favour to the blessed, by the interesting of that dignity wherewith God hath invested the priest, and ingaging of God's own power and institution for a blessing.[1]

The purpose of this book so far has been to ask what we are doing when we bless something, or someone or somewhere. I might have begun by posing a simple question: 'What effect does a blessing have?' That would have been to frame blessings in terms of their effectiveness from the start. Instead I have postponed that question until now, and with good reason. Our sense of what effect a blessing has would be skewed, perhaps hopelessly, unless we assess it against the background of the full variety of what a blessing might set out to achieve. To put it ridiculously, for the sake of emphasis, if we assumed that the purpose of blessing an object was, for instance, to make it glow in the dark, then our sense of whether blessings are 'efficacious'

---

1 George Herbert, *The Country Parson*, Ch. 36, punctuation modernized.

would be couched in a very particular way and lead to a disappointing answer.

The question of what effect blessings have lies close to the origins of this book. For five months I lived, prayed and studied with the seminarians at the Venerable English College in Rome as part of an exchange between the Roman Catholic Church and the Church of England.[2] As part of this I enrolled at the Angelicum, the Dominican university in Rome, and studied several courses. Worthy of particular praise was the introduction to sacramental theology taught by the prior. An earlier book of mine, *Why Sacraments?*, no doubt bears the trace of those lectures.

The lectures were of double length so we were given a break in the middle. Since I got on well with the prior I would often find myself in the university bar drinking an espresso with him. On one occasion the first half of his lecture had covered the subject of blessings. In general the lecture course had provided a cogent and devout doctrine of the sacraments, which I received gladly, but his account of blessing worried me. It was as if praising the sacraments inevitably meant playing down everything else. Blessings are not sacraments, so the prior had tended to stress what blessings are *not*: not being sacraments, they are not guaranteed; they do not unite us to Christ; they do not leave a lasting stamp upon our soul, and so on. Sacraments are efficacious and, by this comparative logic, blessings are not.

In the bar, over my espresso, I outlined my concern with friendly forcefulness: his account of blessings, I said, was 'empty and Zwinglian' (after the Genevan Reformer, Zwingli, who of all the mainstream Protestant Reformers had most

---

2 It is a valuable but strange sort of exchange in that it only ever operates in one direction: from Canterbury to Rome and back again, never the other way round.

discounted the supernatural efficacy of the sacraments, leaving them rather like enacted sermon illustrations). 'I would rather', replied the prior, 'be "empty and Zwinglian" than magical and superstitious.' There we stood, with smiles on our faces, he, the Roman Catholic, branded by me as 'Zwinglian' and I, from the Church of England, branded by him as 'superstitious'. That exchange suggested to me that the theology of blessing was a significant subject, that it bore directly on the worshipping life of most Christians and that little had been written about it that ran to any length and was reasonably accessible. This book, with all its faults, is the result.

I propose in this chapter to explore two angles on the efficacy of blessings. The first is to look back over what we have already said that blessings involve or seek to achieve; the second is to ask how a blessing 'changes things' in any further way. From a survey of what we have already seen that blessings can mean, we can start by saying that they are a form of thanksgiving. With a blessing we acknowledge that what we have before us comes from God, whether we are talking about some object or place, some person or persons or some situation. If a blessing serves to acknowledge God, and if it elicits thankfulness from the participants, then it is effective on those terms. That can be understood, in part, in terms of the internal life of those involved: their thankfulness to God, their understanding of the world, and so on. That inner and individual aspect, however, is not all. A blessing is almost always some form of *public* act, and such an act of acknowledging and thanking has public effect – it is therefore effective in that way also.

From acknowledgement and thanksgiving we can move on to blessings as praise. Blessings are 'effective' acts of personal and corporate praise, both for the Church met together in private and as declarations of God's glory in the public square, depending on where the blessing happens. Praise is peculiarly directed to God; it is pre-eminently a moment when we are forgetful of self and attentive to the Almighty. That cautions us against reducing our assessment of the efficacy of blessing to the achievement of some effect in the world that is favourable for us. Such concerns are not insignificant, such assessments not irrelevant, but they are certainly not all. Such a focus would be positively deleterious if it deflects us from seeing and seeking God as all-in-all.

Efficacy, then, means more than achieving some sort of advantage for ourselves in the world; blessing is far more than some imminent manipulation of the forces of the world for the sake of our own goals. That is not to say that we should turn our back on the sense that blessings achieve something in the world. For one thing, as we have just noticed, they achieve an acknowledgement of God, thankfulness and praise. These are all good things to seek, both for the sake of our own particular Christian discipleship and for the sake of the witness they offer to the wider world.

Blessings are also part of the way the liturgy is forever reconstituting the Church and reminding the Christian community of what it is. Edward Kilmartin made this comment about all of Christian worship: not the least part of its 'efficacy' is to gather and renew the Church. It 'recalls the original action of Christ and his followers, by which the Church was founded and the meaning of membership determined'.[3] The common worshipping life of the Church carries on that work of gathering and holding in shape:

As [a] communicative activity, the Christian liturgy brings to the surface of consciousness of the participants the gifts which are already given with the life of faith: the saving

---

3 Edward Kilmartin, *Christian Liturgy: 1. Theology* (Kansas City, MO: Sheed & Ward, 1988), p. 41.

presence of God, personal union with Christ in the Church by means of the power of the Holy Spirit.

Blessing is one part of this 'bringing to the surface of consciousness', both individual and collective. It is an ongoing part of an ongoing liturgy, which is forever renewed since 'the members of the Church live in and through history and so must continually celebrate their common life of faith lest they lose the awareness of their identity.'

Blessings remind us of truths that we could do well to remember: they are effective, therefore, as *teaching*, whether that is to hold the nature of the Church before us or the significance of the world as God's creation, as fallen but orientated to God and being redeemed, and as the arena of our salvation. Blessing also directs our attention to the world around us in a way that is conscious of the inherent overlap of materiality and significance, and reminds us that the physical and the spiritual are far from distinct terms.

One of the few discussions of the efficacy of blessing to have been produced by my own, Anglican, tradition is found in a report of the Church of England's Doctrine Commission, published in 1971 as an exploration of the relationship between baptism and the blessing of infants outside of the rites of baptism.[4] The relevant section is worth reproducing at length. It takes as its starting point the idea of asking anyone around us for his or her blessing:

When we ask a man [*sic*] for his blessing, we ask him to express a favourable attitude towards us and our doings. He is saying that he is for us, and not against us, and

---

4 Archbishops' Commission on Christian Doctrine, *Baptism, Thanksgiving and Blessing* (London: General Synod of the Church of England, 1971), chaired by Ian Ramsey, then Bishop of Durham.

that our good is his good. It follows that there is a strong optative [the grammatical mood for the expression of hope] overtone to blessing, 'May things go well with you', together with a more mutual suggestion of material help. If I have given my blessing to a project, I am likely to help it along as opportunity occurs: we shower blessings on the bride and bridegroom in the form of wedding presents as well as good wishes.

This can act as an analogy for what it means for us to ask for God's blessing:

God's blessing is basically the expression of God's goodwill towards us. God is on our side, our good is his good, and this fact is spelled out in the words addressed to us for our benefit when the blessing is pronounced in his name by bishop or priest. To the questions 'What happens when a person is blessed?' or 'What difference does it make?' the first answer is that the mind of God is made manifest: God's goodwill towards that person has been expressed in words so that it can be communicated to man.

This does not mean that we have changed God's mind. Rather, we have asked more explicitly for God to be involved, and we have borne witness to God's goodness:

It is not supposed that before the blessing there was a lack of goodwill, any more than that before I gave my blessing to a scheme, I disapproved of it. I may have approved of it all along and have been going to help it in due course; the only difference there is as a result of my giving my blessing is that I have said that I approve. And, similarly, the only thing that the pronouncement of God's blessing necessarily effects is that God's will, already well-disposed towards us, has now been made explicit in words. At the same time, in asking God's blessing for a person, there is an element of petition. We are asking God to do well by that person. We are not saying specifically what sort of good things are desired, although often somewhat limited and tangible goods are the ones really being sought. Christians regard these as peripheral although real, and reckon that the greatest goods are the gifts of grace . . . what [we] will get, if [we] allow God to give [us] the best gift He can give to any man, is Jesus Christ himself.[5]

The word 'only' here ('the *only* thing that the pronouncement of God's blessing necessarily effects is that God's will . . . has now been made explicit in words') may be a little reductive, but on the whole this report was otherwise and usefully non-reductive, suggesting some of the purposes that blessing might achieve.

What Does Blessing Change?

Blessings are reminders and they help us to remember the element of risk in our lives and the fragility of human beings, relationship and objects. There is an admirable directness to wanting a blessing before setting out on a journey, especially if there is some element of danger involved. Does a blessing, then, keep the traveller safe? Does it protect the car? Does it preserve a child from harm? Is the church synod that begins with a blessing on its activities more likely to come to a good decision? Am I less likely to contract food poisoning if I say grace? With these questions we

---

5 Archbishops' Commission, *Baptism, Thanksgiving and Blessing*, §11.

move beyond surveying the efficacy of blessings in terms of all that we have already covered in this book, to consider that other dimension, which will rightly not go away and which can incompletely but not inaccurately be phrased as 'But does blessing *change* anything?'

The answer we give to that question will be the same as our answer to the question about the efficacy of prayer in general. Here we encounter the Achilles heel of those Christians who wish to run the efficacy of blessings down, perhaps because they are not (always) sacraments. In the last analysis a blessing is, at least, a prayer. As Simon Chan puts it, 'words of benediction' – here referring to the blessing at the end of the Eucharist – is intended as more than a pious 'wish'. We might therefore go beyond that Church of England report, which talked about blessings in terms of hope (in the 'optative' mood), to cast them as something a little more definite (in what the grammarians would call the 'indicative' mood).[6]

A blessing is a prayer, and most Christians have confidence in the efficacy of prayer – as do many other people besides, including otherwise very much 'lapsed' or 'nominal' Christians. Blessings are prayers, materially enacted. If we have any sense that prayers are worth making, then blessings are also worth performing, *as prayers*. Indeed, blessings are a rather special sort of prayer in that they often have some official sanction by which our prayer is taken up into the prayer of the whole Church. That is one of the benefits of using approved liturgies for these sorts of celebrations or rites: if we bless a house, a grave or a journey with a prayer that is used by Christians around the world and bears some sort of approbation from the

---

6 Simon Chan, *Liturgical Theology: The Church as Worshipping Community* (Downers Grove, IL: InterVarsity Press, 2006), p. 146.

authorities of the Church, then we make our local celebration more than local. We should always pray in solidarity with Christians of all times and places; the formality of a blessing can make that particularly obvious.

What is Anything?

Where we go with the question of what blessing changes will depend on where we start – on the parameters and assumptions that govern our thought from the beginning. In her book *The Mystery of Sacrifice*, Evelyn Underhill described blessing, or consecration, in relation to the perfection of a thing:

> Consecration is a creative act. It does not merely mean taking something that is already complete in itself, and applying it unchanged to a new purpose: but making it that which indeed it should be, and has not yet become.[7]

Consecration is a transformative act. An item or person is not simply put to new work while remaining invariant itself. Nor should we say that it is simply *understood* differently and suppose that this amounts to rather little, as if what something is and how it features in the world and in the human imagination are totally independent. That sort of separation, of brute facts from overlaid meanings, buys into the assumption that all that anything really amounts to is so much inert stuff, and since that is as true after a blessing as before, nothing on that view will have changed. The

---

7 Evelyn Underhill, *The Mystery of Sacrifice* (London: Longmans, Green & Co., 1938), p. 43.

Christian, however, would have good reason not to cede the world and its meanings – or supposed lack of them – to the reductive materialists in this way. The object in front of us, which we meet to bless, is not simply so much stuff: it is a youth centre; it is an altar; it is a human being. Each of those things already inhabits the world of meanings; that is part of what and how it is. Meaning is already integral, so if we change its meaning we change part of what it is. Everything is already partly constituted by its relations, not least because – going further – everything is *entirely* constituted as what it is by virtue of its relation to God.

Underhill went on:

> The consecrated church [building], already a convenient place of worship, enters the supernatural order and becomes a sanctuary of the Spirit, a house of prayer. The consecrated life, already useful and devoted, obedient to the commandments, becomes by its total self-giving an instrument of the action of God. So the consecration of the Eucharist takes the gifts of bread and wine and lifts them up into a new sphere of reality; makes them something which they were not before . . . It brings home to us the plastic . . . half-finished character of the physical world; the fact that it points beyond itself and awaits at every level transformation in God, in order to achieve completeness through the quickening action of His supernatural life.[8]

---

8 Underhill, *Mystery of Sacrifice*, pp. 43–4. I have omitted the words 'half-real', since it strikes me as a theological mistake to say that the openness of anything makes it less real, or that its dependence on God does, for that matter. God is the whole origin of all things; they exist only by his gift but his gift is that they should truly, although derivatively, *be*. I discuss this in my book *Participation* (Eugene, OR: Wipf & Stock, 2014).

Everything in the world is a work in progress, and everything has a certain boundlessness about it; things are poised always to exceed what they currently are, in some direction that is continuous with their current natures but also goes beyond it. Part of why anything can be *more* in this way is that it can come to be known and loved, can feature in some larger story or drama and can enter into relation with other things.[9] This is part of what blessing effects and achieves. We could say that something 'flowers' or 'blooms' through being known or loved, on entering into a wider story and being related to other things. This view reminds us that knowledge, desire, imagination and so on are facts about the world.

We can take the example of a tree. In one sense a tree is not changed by being known, celebrated, blessed or whatever. Its matter remains the same, and that tends to be the aspect of the tree with which the scientist concerns him- or herself, for instance. This aspect is part of the full picture but not the whole of it. A claim that the universe consists only of matter is simply false. Thoughts, desires and stories are also part of the universe; so is personhood, love and goodness. The meaning of something is a real aspect. The tree at the bottom of a garden, which has featured in the life of three generations of a family, has certain meanings on that account. Statements such as 'this is the tree under which Sam and Ruth were engaged' or 'this is the only tree around here that survived the storm of 2012' are statements about the tree and not just about human consciousness. To take this to its furthest extreme, we might consider the fragments of wood preserved in the church of Santa Croce in Rome, which are taken by most of the

---

9 To use Aristotle's terminology, things accumulate accidents, and relation is an accident.

world's Christians to be parts of the cross on which Jesus was crucified. Only the most reductive of materialists could claim that these are just any old piece of wood (and even if they turned out, historically, not to be relics of the true cross, they would have a certain, non-arbitrary significance all the same, as objects of reverence for at least a millennium and a half).

Drawing on these sorts of ideas we can say that the blessing of a person, thing or place positions it anew, such that it is now understood differently. There is a new element to its story, which has to be told for it to be fully apprehended. Or to put it another way, this person, thing or place is drawn into a changed pattern of relationships to other people and things, within the Christian community and within the wider community, since that act of blessing is a public fact as well as an ecclesial one.

I remember reading a Facebook post in which a priest uploaded a photograph of the container he proposed to use to bring the holy oils back from the annual Eucharist at which they are blessed by the bishop. The container was unusual since it had originally been designed as a hip flask for carrying three different types of spirit. An inquisitive – and not hostile – respondent asked what difference such a blessing made. The priest replied that such a blessing changed the meaning of the oils because it changed their relationship to God. That may sound minimal but it could also be on to something profoundly important, especially if we consider that something's whole being is grounded in, and flows from, its relationship to God.

Usually the best approach to answering a question is to search for the deep account of what is going on that will undergird other responses, which seem valid in their way but also incomplete. We need not dismiss them for being partial, for all they are partial, especially if we can see what they each rest upon. Taken by itself, the suggestion that blessing changes things simply by 'changing their meaning' would be partial at best. If, however, we extend that to say that blessing puts something in a new relationship to God, then we have gone much further. Indeed, we have said what may be most fundamental for understanding blessing: there is a new meaning not simply because human beings have ascribed an enlarged significance to something but rather because we recognize a new meaning in relation to God.

When we bless something we change its orientation. We direct it towards God, not so as to imply that it was not already God's or that God was not already the One in whom the fulfilment of all things is to be found, but so as to make this explicit and, in a certain sense, to underline it. Blessing has always had some aspect to it of consecration or setting apart, and this is part of its 'effect'. We do not treat a blessed object or person, or anything else, in quite the same way as it was before. Part of this change of relationship, as we have said, has a human reference: the object, person or place now inhabits the human world – or is inhabited – in a different sort of way. It has been taken up into the collective imagination and into collective intention in a different way from before. We could make an analogy with the 'anathema' or exclusion from the Church that we looked at in Chapter 5. To be anathema is to be cut off from the Church, one hopes for a short while, and for one's relation to God to be interrupted; not indeed that any existing thing can be 'disconnected' from God as the cause of its existence but rather that its orientation to God as goal is impeded, not least in terms of the ongoing work of grace fulfilling nature. If cursing – anathema – is about being cut off, then blessing, by analogy, is about incorporation and relation. If, on the one hand, how a place or thing – and certainly a person – features in relation to others is partly constitutive of what it is, then the way anything relates to God is *entirely* constitutive of its being.

For an account of the nature of things as grounded in their relation to God, the most obvious place to turn might be to a vision drawn from Augustine and Aquinas, first of all cultivated by Roman Catholics but also taken up by many others.[10] We might, however, also think of some recent work on the thought of Martin Luther that has stressed the extent to which ideas of 'place' undergird that Reformer's metaphysics. Jon Mackenzie argues that Luther understood justification as a 'replacement' not in the sense of rubbing the thing out and 'replacing' it with something else but of placing it in a new 'location' in relation to God – and where one stands in relation to God is no trifling matter. Using that language we could say that blessing reconfigures something in relation to God by 'replacing it' – placing it before God in a new way, in a new location.[11]

Not for nothing, perhaps, do prayers and rites of blessing make use of this imagery of 'placing before God', sometimes in words but more often in gesture. Consider the Church of England's most recent reworking of a set of prayers at the eucharistic offertory that go back to the time of Jesus: 'Blessed are you, Lord God of all creation, through your goodness we have this bread/this wine *to set before you* . . .' In the realm of gesture, placing is often a highly important part of a rite of blessing (although this may go unnoticed), whether that involves placing something upon the altar or setting it down somewhere else – however it is that, in this location, we naturally express

---

10 For an example of this, see my *Participation*.

11 Jon Mackenzie, 'Luther's Topology: *Creatio Ex Nihilo* and the Cultivation of the Concept of Place in Martin Luther's Theology', *Modern Theology* 29 (2013), pp. 83–103.

'setting something before God'. Even the impulse to bring something or someone into church for the blessing is a tacit expression of the significance of 'placing' as part of a rite of blessing.

However we work this out, the idea that blessing reorientates or underlines a relation to God stands as one of the most potent underpinnings for an entire theology of blessing. It is also an ideal place to begin accounting for how blessing changes that which is blessed. Another central aspect is that blessing, like other prayers, calls us to action. It is to that idea we now turn.

8

Blessing, Action and the Natural Order

A challenge in any discussion of the action of God in the world, such as ours in this book, is not to divorce the extraordinary work of God from his ordinary work, not to contrast grace with nature in such a way as to exclude each from the other, nor to suppose that theology only takes off when explanations that could be given by any other discipline – sociology, for instance, or psychology – have come to an end. We can appreciate the value of blessings in terms of some extraordinary dedication to God or in terms of a prayer for God's special intervention in the world. None of that would be wrong in itself but it would be unhelpful if it was thought to stand in disjunction to the way God's world operates 'usually'. As an analogy, we might say of the sacraments that they are profound channels for the grace of God and are the best ways we have to live beyond a this-world-only logic. In that way they might feature in our pastoral care as graced ways in which we open ourselves up to God or God opens us up to himself. That would be true, but we would be making a theological mistake if we took this to imply that the worldly, immanent dimension of the sacraments is therefore inconsequential: the dimension upon which the sociologist or the psychologist might wish to comment. God, after all, is the cause of the natural order as well as the supernatural order; God is 'found' in the natural order as well as beyond it. Taking up that point about pastoral care, we would not be demeaning the sacraments to talk about the ways in which any number of the 'natural' capacities of the sacramental rites also serve the pastoral ministry. We might consider, for instance, that they are occasions for human contact, for teaching, for a communal marking of something that is important; or that they provide a liturgical structure that can 'hold' a highly charged event or situation. To mark and celebrate any of this is not to deny grace. These 'worldly' dimensions are not the whole picture but they are part of it. Grace does not come, in the sacraments, in contradistinction to any way in which those sacraments are naturally helpful; grace comes, in part, through those aspects too.

All, therefore, that has just been said about sacraments applies to blessings (and to any other material, symbolic act of prayer and worship that, while not a sacrament in itself, clearly inhabits adjoining territory; these rites are often called sacramentals). There is a human, natural cultural dimension to what is going on when we bless something. While that is not the whole picture it is part of it, and whatever else we might want to say about God's operation in a blessing going beyond a natural, immanent picture, it is not disjointed from that picture. As Edward Kilmartin put it (with the sacraments in mind): to say that 'a divine intervention occurs in favour of the participants' does not stop the event having the character of 'any authentic human engagement'.[1] Any action of God that goes beyond what is 'naturally' comprehensible is not some extraneous overlay, not least because God was already at work in whatever is

---

[1] Edward Kilmartin, *Christian Liturgy: 1. Theology* (Kansas City, MO: Sheed & Ward, 1988), p. 25.

then further elevated, in a way that is not at all comparable with creation's own action: God is God; creatures are creatures. On account of that, the involvement of God in anything human and creaturely does not make it less human or creaturely. Indeed, the work of God is always to perfect and sanctify; by it things are made more themselves, more what they could be, not less.

If the distinction between the natural and the more than natural is not to be overplayed, we might consider that the character of blessing – and also of curse – is already to be found woven into the order of things. The natural law tradition of ethics, at least at its best, plays upon this point. Samuel Powell, in his book *Participating in God*, draws attention to a passage in the book of Proverbs that enumerates the doleful 'consequences of not paying attention to wisdom' (Prov. 1.24–33).[2] This is followed in Proverbs 2 by another passage where those who do pay attention to wisdom are told that they can expect blessing. Such comments have us dealing not so much with what theologians call special providence (which is the territory of miracles) but rather with general providence (which describes the ways the order of what God has created 'provides' for our needs). There are 'miraculous' blessings – and miraculous curses for that matter. They are not in view here. We are talking about blessings and curses in the structure of the world. As Powell puts it:

According to the Old Testament, creatures have a share in God's wisdom. They participate in it. On one hand, participation in wisdom appears in the order of nature – the seasons and rhythms of nature, the earth's provision

---

2 Samuel M. Powell, *Participating in God: Creation and Trinity* (Minneapolis, MN: Fortress Press, 2003), p. 43.

for life, and so on. On the other hand, wisdom has a special meaning for humans, where it appears as the moral law of cause and effect, a law that humans can participate in to their blessing or resist to their destruction.[3]

To put this in familiar but potentially uncomfortable terms: we reap what we sow. This is a principle we can uphold in general, although it can certainly be put to blunt and self-righteous use and is not without problems, especially in relation to specific cases. That is reason to be cautious but not to dismiss the idea without a further look.

The proposal here is that God has established an order to the nature of things; it is for our good provision but can turn to our detriment if ignored. Something, broadly speaking, of blessing, and of curse, already lies in the recompense for good or ill that comes from our interaction with nature.

We should admit, to take an example, that someone living respectfully towards the world, at least in comparison to others, can contract hepatitis from a blood transfusion. We need not and should not say that they are specifically receiving the judgement of God. Similarly, those who suffer most from the effects of pollution are rarely those most responsible for producing it. Such observations indicate the need for caution – not least pastoral caution – in discussing these questions. Individual cases do not necessarily follow a general trend. All the same, links exist between how we live and how that life has an impact on us; there are trends, woven into the fabric of things. If we take a step back, patterns begin to emerge.[4] Temperance makes sense, for instance: it is 'wise' to live moderately, to pick up the

---

3 Powell, *Participating in God*, p. 43.

4 The mathematicians would say that there is a relation at work here, only that it is a *stochastic* rather than a deterministic one.

language of the book of Proverbs. Eat a balanced diet and, by and large, your health will be better than if you do not, which is a blessing; make sure you are active for at least an hour each day and you are likely to live longer. From the perspective of wider society, the links are even stronger (since the patterns emerge most of all on aggregate). To return to an earlier example, a society that invests in good screening of donated blood will reap the consequences in fewer infections, which is a blessing. Indeed, the more fundamental feature of access to blood transfusions *at all* is part of the blessing that accrues from having invested in scientific research in the first place and in a good healthcare system.

If these examples rancour left-leaning readers – and I am a left-leaning writer – then such a reader would be correct to point to a wider arena for blessing and curse, in the realm of how a whole society orders itself. A host of examples could be given: the curse that comes upon the environment when we despoil it for our own short-term advantage would be one. Or we might consider the international economic situation in the years leading up to the publication of this book, which similarly displays a profound sense of 'cursedness', linked to our current financial order, or disorder.

A pattern of blessing, then, is woven into the fabric of reality and revealed when we act towards it with wisdom; and a pattern of curse when we act towards it foolishly. Like other aspects of blessing discussed in this book, it is just that: an aspect. We cannot reduce the whole topic to this facet but neither should we discount it as part of what might properly be said. When a person or a society does not prosper, that *can* be because of an unwise way of life. Such an association is part of the biblical witness. We need not see this as a curse descending out of the blue from God. It is mediated by the way things are. The bigger picture is that God has blessed us with a planet that provides more than enough for all, but if we live greedy lives, if we run our common life on principles of debt, if we live more by the abstractions of financial instruments (so complex they cannot be understood or modelled) than by the tangible fruits of the earth and labour, then the blessing turns sour.

Blessing and Action

A further connection between the human and the divine action comes with the observation that we should both pray and try to be part of the answer to our own prayers as much as is feasible. Shane Claiborne and Jonathan Wilson-Hartgrove said something important about prayer – although not all of it – when they wrote that 'Prayer is not so much about convincing God to do what we want God to do as it is about convincing ourselves to do what God wants us to do.'[5] That principle applies to blessings as much as it does to any other form of prayer. Blessing does not absolve us from action; it commits us to it.

Blessing is a sort of proclamation, and we are dull-hearted if, having witnessed a new relationship of some thing or person to God, we carry on as we did before. Moreover, in as much as an act of blessing is a consecration, there should be an even stronger commitment on our part to treat a person, thing or activity with a new disposition of heart. We need only think of a marriage, ordination or lay commissioning, or of the blessing of a church building or of vessels for the Eucharist, or of a church homeless project. In each case the blessing is self-consciously a beginning, not a conclusion. Each is a moment when we resolve to treat certain people,

---

5 Shane Claiborne and Jonathan Wilson-Hartgrove, *Becoming the Answer to Our Prayers: Prayer for Ordinary Radicals* (Downers Grove, IL: InterVarsity Press, 2008), p. 11.

things or situations with what a philosopher might call a new 'intentionality'. That is to say, we relate in a new way towards them: the root of 'intention' is the Latin *tendere*, meaning to stretch (towards) or even to crane the neck.

Serious attention to intentionality led to a – slow – revolution in philosophy;[6] in a vaguely parallel fashion, the idea of intentionality has also done much to revitalize Christian discipleship in the past couple of decades.[7] The paradigm example is of the 'intentional community', where a group of people make mutual commitments to live together after Christian pattern. The idea of intentionality has wider application whenever we realize that the Christian journey is one that requires resolve,[8] and that the greatest joys often come through making particular commitments to particular people.[9] Situations in which we particularly want to bless something, someone or a group of people, line up closely with the situations where the intentionality of Christian discipleship comes particularly to the fore. That might mark the

---

6 The modern story starts with Franz Brentano (1838–1917), who championed the significance of the idea, and proceeds through the phenomenologists – Edmund Husserl (1859–1938), Martin Heidegger (1889–1976), Maurice Merleau-Ponty (1908–61) – into the present day.

7 Ivan J. Kauffman has written a survey of the idea of intentionality in Christian thought and life entitled *Follow Me: A History of Christian Intentionality* (Eugene, OR: Wipf & Stock, 2009).

8 I am using the word 'intention' here in its colloquial sense, which is close to 'resolve'. Intentionality has a wider meaning in philosophy, with a more general sense of one thing being directed towards another. In a now somewhat classic definition, Pierre Jacob defined intentionality as 'the power of minds to be about, to represent, or to stand for, things, properties and states of affairs' ('Intentionality', in *The Stanford Encyclopedia of Philosophy*, Fall 2010 edition, edited by Edward N. Zalta, http://plato. stanford.edu/archives/fall2010/entries/intentionality/). That broader understanding relates to other aspects of blessing, as for instance when we mean a blessing as an act of praise, reorientation or teaching.

9 I have written about that, in relation to marriage, in *Why Sacraments?* (London: SPCK/Eugene, OR: Wipf & Stock, 2013), pp. 110–11.

beginning of a common resolve, as with a marriage, in setting up a community or other common Christian venture, or in setting aside a building to be used in a particular way. In an ongoing sense, blessings can recognize intentionality when they touch upon something that lies close to the heart of that unfolding life, as when we bless food at our common meals, day by day. Blessing and intentionality are also central at moments when we recommit ourselves, such as at the renewal of wedding vows or at a service to mark a particular anniversary in the life of a community.

A salutary example of the relation between blessing and intentionality is provided by the 'New Age' writer David Spangler. When he sounded out his friends on the topic of blessing, one replied, 'I bless my house by appreciating it and caring for it.'[10] We might write this response off as banal or offer the theological critique that since Spangler's book is concerned with the esoteric manipulation of psychic 'energies', we would not expect to find anything other than this sort of 'immanent' reference for blessing. We should not, however, be too easily dismissive here: 'appreciating . . . and caring' may not be the whole of blessing but they are certainly a part. Active care and appreciation are part of recognition and thanksgiving, even if they are not everything blessing can be. Although the Christian notion of blessing goes further, a Christian blessing should, all the same, certainly lead to 'appreciation . . . and caring'. We might return to that example of the blessing of a home, especially one's own home. We would not have entered into all that a blessing is supposed to mean if we had our home blessed and then studiously neglected it.

---

10 David Spangler, *Blessing: The Art and the Practice* (New York: Riverhead Books, 2001), p. 285.

Blessings, then, are prayers already particularly closely aligned with action. Just as we pray and seek to live in a way that is consistent with bringing about what we pray for, so we bless and seek to live in a way that aligns with the purpose of that blessing, dedication or consecration. This illustrates the natural alignment between the more 'supernatural' and the more 'natural' senses of the word 'bless' or 'blessing'. We ought not to despise the ways – such as simple human kindness – in which we can be a blessing by 'natural' means, not least because the distinction between natural and supernatural, or between nature and grace, is a difficult one to draw, and perhaps not one we should want to police too closely. Nature is always already graced, not least because it is gift, and grace is worked out in the arena of natural things: the humanity of Jesus of Nazareth and those before and after him, the nails and the wood of the cross, and so on.

Having said all that, we should also acknowledge a danger in such thought about human action: we might suppose it all depends on us and become either proud, despairing or exhausted. Here, however, the practice and theology of blessing itself comes to our aid since blessing is precisely an action where we wait upon the action of God. As Evelyn Underhill put it, blessing teaches us that 'It is God alone who is the mover, the doer of all that is done. He alone uplifts, renews, transforms, converts, [and] consecrates.'[11]

In this comment Underhill may, in fact, set divine action and human action a little too far apart. Precisely as unutterably different, they can be intimately intertwined – as we have seen in this chapter.[12]

---

11 Evelyn Underhill, *The Mystery of Sacrifice* (London: Longmans, Green & Co., 1938), p. 44.

12 On this, see the chapter on participation in divine action in my *Participation* (Eugene, OR: Wipf & Stock, 2014).

9

Varieties of Blessing
(and not Blessing)

The liturgical practices of the Western churches today are strongly influenced by a reform movement that swept the churches in the twentieth century. We could properly associate it with the Second Vatican Council but its roots lie further back in the twentieth century and it should be seen as a set of parallel and interrelated reforms, including traditions that reach beyond the Roman Catholic Church. Those reforms have affected how we think about blessings, both in terms of what happens within church services and what happens outside them, for instance at home. Put in a nutshell, the trend when it comes to blessing things has been paradoxical, or at least bizarre: it has been to move away from blessing them.

Varieties of Blessings

To aid this discussion we need some terminology and some back-story. The Christian tradition has long seen blessing as operating in more than one way or at more than one level. Not every sort of blessing should be thought to be doing the same sort of thing and, in particular, blessings come in different levels of solemnity. The terminology for these distinctions is somewhat loose, and what a particular word means in a given case is best gauged by what it is set against by way of contrast. A distinguished distinction is between *consecration* and *blessing*.[1] A consecration, in this sense, is synonymous with a *dedication*, and that highlights what is distinctive about it: it dedicates, or places, something *outside* 'ordinary' (or 'secular') usage. In contrast, when something is *blessed* it is blessed so that it can fulfil its role *within* everyday life.[2] We could take buildings as an example. A house is *blessed* in view of its role as a dwelling for human beings and a setting for human life; a church is dedicated or *consecrated* so as to make it a place outside the ordinary run of things: a house of God and of prayer. We should note that 'secular' here has nothing to do with atheism or being unreligious. Derived from the Latin word for 'the world' (*saeculum*), it simply means 'pertaining to the world', without any sense that the order of the world is not a religious one or that it stands in any way in contradistinction to God.

'Secular' use is what a house is all about, and the act of blessing it helps us to criticize any sense of the 'secular' that opposes it to God or assumes that things of the world are spiritually neutral. We can cheerfully do everything in a blessed house that pertains to a human life, approached from a Christian perspective. That is what *blessing* is about. In contrast, according to this ancient distinction, performing 'secular' activities in a *consecrated* church would be an act of 'desecration': that might include holding a corporate board meeting, for instance, or turning it over to a nightclub on Saturday evenings. That is not because 'secular' activities are wrong in themselves. They are not sinful for being

---

1 Herbert Vorgrimler, *Sacramental Theology* (Collegeville, MN: Liturgical Press, 1992), p. 316.

2 Mark Drew, 'Introduction', in Sean Finnegan (ed.), *Consecrations, Blessings and Prayers* (London: Canterbury Press, 2005), p. xi.

secular and, in as much as anything is sinful, a blessing no more opens the way for it than a consecration would. It is just that, all this said, consecration puts a building aside. Its dedication bears witness to a destiny that is not necessarily antithetical to the way of the world but which certainly goes beyond it.[3] Another example might be drawn from the dedication or consecration of people. Following New Testament examples, the Church has recognized the dedication of virgins and widows since earliest times. For someone who has taken this vow, marriage would be a desecration – not because marriage is wrong in itself, far from it, but because this person has made a voluntary vow to live in a different manner of life.

This is not an entirely inflexible picture. Most churches that operate with a vital sense of consecration also understand that such consecrations can be dissolved or removed – usually, in these situations, by a bishop. The person who is vowed to celibacy but wishes to marry can ask for the vow to be set aside through the authority of the Church. This is a better way to proceed than carrying on regardless, since it avoids the 'scandal' of publicly breaking a solemn vow.

Many churches observe something of this distinction between consecration and blessing. It is often reflected in the sense of who the right *minister* might be for a particular sort of 'blessing', with consecration reserved to bishops. This is reflected in Anglican practice, for instance, as well as in the Roman Catholic Church, with bishops associated with the consecration of churches, altars and bells, for instance.[4]

---

3 As the Roman Catholic *Code of Canon Law* puts it: 'Sacred objects, which are designated for divine worship by dedication or blessing, are to be treated reverently and are not to be employed for profane or inappropriate use even if they are owned by private persons' (canon 1171).

4 Bells are an unusual case. Traditionally, their dedication includes elements akin to a baptism.

To say this is to explore a distinction between consecration and blessing. Much the same contrast is sometimes made – perhaps confusingly – by talking about two different sorts of blessing. Using this terminology, the consecration/blessing distinction maps, instead, onto two different categories of blessing: *constitutive* blessings and *invocative* blessings.[5] Constitutive blessings are what we earlier called consecrations (or dedications). They change how we use something, they set it aside for God because they affect the thing, place or person itself.[6] In contrast, invocative blessings ask for God's favour in relation to a thing, person or place but do not dedicate it for a purpose beyond ordinary use. Most blessings are likely to be invocative. In Roman Catholic theology, a constitutive blessing is said to possess an objectivity and effectiveness that come from the objectivity and efficacy of the prayer of the Church, taken as a whole. In contrast, as Uwe Lang puts it, the effect of an invocative blessing 'depends on the fervor of the recipient and on the will of God'.[7]

---

5 In Latin the distinction is between *benedictiones constitutivae* and *benedictiones invocatvae*.

6 Uwe Lang notes that this is the category under discussion in the *Catechism of the Catholic Church* (London: Burns & Oates, 2004; see also www.vatican.va/archive/ENG0015/_INDEX.HTM), §1672, although the term 'constitutive blessing' is not used – Uwe Michael Lang, 'Theologies of Blessing: Origins and Characteristics of *De benedictionibus* (1984)', *Antiphon* 15.1 (2011), p. 34.

7 Lang, 'Theologies of Blessing', p. 34. There is a further contrast to be made here, which is with the sacraments: the efficacy of an invocative blessing is in the hands of the pious *recipient*, the efficacy of a constitutive blessing rests rather more on the one *performing* the act (namely on the Church and its prayer, taken as a whole, within which the blessing is said to lodge), although ultimately on God in both cases, and the efficacy of a sacrament rests so directly upon God that the emphasis is not so much on the objectivity of the Church, through which God acts, but on the objectivity of the action itself. (Constitutive) blessings, that is, act by virtue of the one who performs them (which is put in Latin as *ex opera operantis*

For the sake of completeness, we might note that this twofold distinction – either between consecration and blessing or between constitutive blessings and invocative blessings – has been expanded in the contemporary Roman Catholic Church since the revisions of canon law that led to the new *Code of Canon Law* in 1983. That code offers a fourfold distinction,[8] resembling a hybrid of our consecration/blessing and constitutive/invocative terminologies. A first group of blessings lie on the left-hand side of these distinctions (that is to say, with 'consecration' or 'constitutive blessings'). Two of them, the most solemn, involve anointing: the consecration of *people* and the dedication of *places and things*.[9] A consecration or dedication with anointing is the most solemn of these rites. A consecrated person might be an abbot or abbess; a dedicated place might be a church, and a dedicated thing an altar. The third sort of blessing is a constitutive blessing without anointing. An example might be the blessing of a chalice for use at the Eucharist. In contemporary Roman Catholic usage, each of these three actions – for example, the blessing of an abbess, altar or chalice – would be the work of the bishop or of a priest who has been given permission by the bishop. In Anglican custom the blessings with anointing would probably be reserved to the bishop but not those without anointing: the consecration

---

Ecclesiae – 'by [the power of the] Church's work [of intercession]'). In contrast, sacraments act simply by virtue of the act itself (which is put in Latin as *ex opera operato* – 'by the action of the act'). (On this, see the Roman Catholic *Code of Canon Law*, §1166.) If this sounds complicated, the point is that I would answer the question 'How do I know that this church has been blessed?' by saying 'Because the Church prayed for it', whereas I would answer the question 'How do I know that this person was baptized?' by saying 'Because she was baptized'.

8 In the summary given by Vorgrimler, *Sacramental Theology*, p. 317.

9 Here Vorgrimler may be incorrect: anointing is not usually used in the consecration of people, such as at a monastic profession.

of a church is unlikely to be seen as something to delegate to a priest whereas blessing a chalice would quite comfortably be seen as within a priest's general purview. So far, then, we have seen consecrations of things or people with anointing, and the constitutive blessing of things, people or places without anointing, but which still confer some purpose outside everyday life. The fourth category is the *invocative* blessing. As we have seen, that is not about calling things from the mundane purposes of life.

Failing to Bless Things

With this framework in place we can return to that claim made previously, that in the liturgical reforms of the twentieth century the tendency has been to downgrade blessings and indeed to make them less about blessing at all. We can now put that more precisely and more accurately. The trend was to move from a *constitutive* to an *invocative* emphasis, such that the default option was more to bless by way of vague prayer than bless as impartation. Invocative blessings do not have the same objectivity and sense of innate effectiveness as constitutive blessings: invocative blessings rest on the zeal of the person who uses the thing or inhabits the place.

One of the framers of the modern approach to blessing, Pierre-Marie Gy, expressed the avowed intent for the reformed liturgies to move away from the blessing of things and places towards the blessing of people: 'blessings should be invoked primarily on persons rather than on things or places', he wrote.[10] Going even further, Gy

---

10 Pierre-Marie Gy, '*Labores coetuum a studiis: De benedictionibus*', *Notitiae* 7 (1971), pp. 123–32. See Lang, 'Theologies of Blessing', p. 35.

wondered whether we should use the verb 'to bless' at all when it comes to objects, although even he had to admit that Christ blessed fish (Mark 8.7).[11]

As a parallel to this, after the reforms, prayers for blessing started to shift away from calling down God's blessing upon things to calling down God's blessing on those who might use the thing in question instead. As an example, a prayer would not bless water but rather pray that those who were sprinkled with it might experience God's blessings or that God would look with favour upon them.[12] This trend is reflected throughout the new official Roman Catholic repository of blessings, the *Book of Blessings*,[13] but is also to be found in the prayers of churches that have followed the Roman Catholic theorists in this regard. As Uwe Lang points out, this 'is in discontinuity not just with the medieval and more recent tradition, but also with the practice of the ancient Church'.[14]

In his short but excellent overview of blessing, Mark Drew has pointed out that this twentieth-century move was not well judged: 'in its zeal to combat the excesses of former times, when certain forms of popular piety doubtless were wont to emphasize sacred objects at the expense of holy living', the new *Book of Blessings* 'ruthlessly chooses to exclude the idea of the sanctification of matter from its purview'.[15]

A reaction to superstition and a magical approach to blessing has been taken too far. Drew's comments about

---

11 See Lang, 'Theologies of Blessing', p. 35.

12 Drew, 'Introduction', p. xiv.

13 International Commission on English in the Liturgy of the Roman Catholic Church, *Book of Blessings* (Collegeville, MN: Liturgical Press, 1989).

14 Lang, 'Theologies of Blessing', p. 45.

15 Drew, 'Introduction', p. xiv.

the relation of this move to wider themes in Christian doctrine and in contemporary life are worth quoting in full:

> At a time when ecumenism has helped us rediscover the worship of the Christian East, with its strong sense of Christ's saving work embracing the whole cosmos, and when people everywhere are waking up to the vital need to respect the environment, this desacralizing of the material world seems to many a regrettable concession to the Enlightenment's 'disenchanting' of the natural universe . . . Indeed, one cannot help but wonder if this rejection of something so natural to Catholic piety has not contributed to the lack of uptake from which the *Book of Blessings* has undoubtedly suffered. Many priests, if they continue to bless objects at all, use the prayers from the old Ritual [the *Rituale Romanum*], and as far as one can tell this has never been forbidden by any authority.[16]

Comments of Cipriano Vaggagini bear upon this theme of (not) blessing and the disenchantment of things. While blessing is opposed to 'pantheism, polytheism, magic, naturalism', it is also opposed 'to every kind of secularism'.[17] In rejecting the former, the twentieth-century reformers were in danger of embracing the latter. In fact magic and secularism are surprisingly alike since both approach the world as a closed system. Magic is about the manipulation of powers immanent within the world, without any necessary reference to God. Secularism similarly denies such

---

16 Drew, 'Introduction', pp. xiv–xv. For this reason Sean Finnegan's book *Consecrations, Blessings and Prayers* – of which Drew's essay forms the Introduction – can be particularly recommended since it gives some of those heartier prayers from the old *Rituale Romanum* in dignified modern translations. See also the Bibliography at the end of this book.

17 Drew, 'Introduction', p. xvi.

a reference to God while also denying those immanent powers, or at least the same sort of immanent powers – it necessarily has its own all-prevailing forces, whether of physics or some political system. Blessing, in contrast, opposes both secularism and magic. It opposes secularism by pointing out that the world relates to God, and comes from God, and that it is therefore 'enchanted'; it opposes magic by showing that this 'enchantment' has an origin that lies beyond this world – since the origin of the whole world lies beyond the world, in God – and by insisting that this 'enchantment' is not ours to manipulate.

The Roman Catholic *Book of Blessings* is not the only collection where blessings sometimes do not quite manage to bless what we might be out to bless. The Church of England's modern-language liturgy, *Common Worship*, is notable for having given a more prominent place to certain blessings than previously in the post-Reformation life of the Church of England, as for instance with the blessing of oils by the bishop on Maundy Thursday. However, the texts that the liturgy gives as prayers for these occasions are often not quite up to the job, for the reasons we have been discussing. We might take the blessing of oils as an example. The prayers are theologically fulsome and replete with well-chosen biblical imagery. Here is the prayer over the oil of the sick:

Bishop:
Blessed are you, sovereign God,
gentle and merciful, creator of heaven and earth.
Your Word brought light out of darkness,
and daily your Spirit renews the face of the earth.
Your anointed Son brought healing
to those in weakness and distress.
He broke the power of evil and set us free
    from sin and death

that we might praise your name for ever.
By the power of your Spirit may your blessing rest
on those who are anointed with this oil in your name;
may they be made whole in body, mind and spirit,
restored in your image, renewed in your love,
and serve you as sons and daughters in your kingdom.
Response:
Blessed be God for ever.[18]

This well-constructed prayer falls at the last hurdle when it fails to bless the oil, only asking instead that those who are anointed with the oil may be blessed. The same form of words, 'By the power of your Spirit may your blessing rest on those who are anointed with this oil in your name', occurs in the same place in the prayers over the other two oils.

Using the distinction we encountered above, this prayer is 'invocative', when a full-blooded blessing would be 'constitutive'. In the early twenty-first century such stunted prayers of blessing are common: they are full of eloquence but lacking in courage. We might treat them as useful but incomplete. They are not quite blessings in themselves but work well as instructive prefaces to a fully fledged blessing, which can be appended or inserted.

To pick up the prayer over the oil of the sick, the proposed new translation of the *Roman Pontifical* might be taken as the basis for some suitable words:

Send down from heaven, we pray, your Holy Spirit, the Paraclete, upon this oil, which you were pleased to bring forth from green trees to restore our bodies, so

---

18 *Common Worship: Pastoral Services* (London: Church House Publishing, 2011), pp. 46–7.

that by your holy blessing this oil may be for anyone
who is anointed with it a safeguard for body, mind, and
spirit, to take away every pain, every infirmity, and every
sickness.[19]

These words could be used to 'do the business' after the present
(quasi-) 'blessing' has provided a theological introduction.

On other occasions the task might be for the priest to
search among available options, as when, for instance,
some prayers in the recent Church of England liturgies
bless the water for use in baptism and some do not.

Our liturgies embody our faith. The rule of the Church's
prayer expresses the rule of her faith: *Lex orandi, lex cre-
dendi*, as the Latin formula goes that sums up this idea.
Unobtrusively, prayers and rites of blessing teach a great
deal about what the Church holds to be true about creation, sin, redemption and hope, about the human vocation and the vocation of the rest of creation besides.

The wording of those prayers and rites from the end of
the twentieth century is often poetic and steeped in biblical imagery; it is certainly abundant. All the same, it is
sometimes a little half-hearted and, worse, it can embody
a strange mixture of undue optimism, playing down the
sense in which blessing is part of the way the Church recognizes and faces evil in the world (as we saw in Chapter 5),
and too pessimistic, entertaining Gnostic uneasiness with
blessing material things, forgetting just how much God has
rejoiced to draw material things into the work of salvation
(as we saw in this chapter).

That latter tendency shifts the balance in blessing things
so far towards people and not objects or places that it

19 From www.ibreviary.com/m/preghiere.php?tipo=Rito&id=543,
accessed 23 July 2014, with slight amendment.

forgets that to be human means to be material, to live in places and to interact with objects. *Things* too are part of the human story. In the chapters that follow now in Part 2 of this book, we will consider this further, not least in terms of what we bless, how we bless and what occasions might present themselves when blessing is appropriate and part of the tradition of the Church.

PART 2

Blessing in the Christian Life

10

A Brief History of Blessings in the Life of the Church

Blessings have featured in the lives of Christians since the beginning of the Church.[1] In this second part of the book we will consider some of the ways they may still do so. First, however, it may be useful to present a short history, both of practices of blessing and of attitudes towards them.

The religious outlook of the first Christians had been formed by Judaism, and blessing played an important part in the life of Jewish people in daily, weekly and yearly cycles, both in the temple and at home. Blessings were among the forms of prayer that those early Christians inherited, not least because their primary 'prayer book' was the Psalter, which is full of invocations and ascriptions of blessing, and because the Passover meal, as the precursor of the Eucharist, contained prayers of blessing.

---

1 The starting point of this account is Derek A. Rivard, *Blessing the World: Ritual and Lay Piety in Medieval Religion* (Washington, DC: Catholic University of America Press, 2009). Among other sources I have also used Mark Drew, 'Introduction', in Sean Finnegan (ed.), *Consecrations, Blessings and Prayers* (London: Canterbury Press, 2005) and Uwe Michael Lang, 'Theologies of Blessing: Origins and Characteristics of *De benedictionibus* (1984)', *Antiphon* 15.1 (2011).

Within Jewish traditions today we find particularly developed – and beautiful – patterns of blessing.[2] Christians have much to learn from their Jewish brothers and sisters here. These Jewish prayers have their roots in exclamations of blessing that go back into the time before Christ. We see this in the narrative of the institution of the Last Supper, when Jesus took the bread and 'blessed it' or 'said the blessing' (Mark 14.22; Matt. 26.26). We know the form these prayers would have taken, namely a form known as the Barakah. Many contemporary eucharistic rites include more or less the same prayers as Jesus himself would have used at that moment: 'Blessed are you . . .'. The Barakah pattern begins 'Blessed are you, Lord God, King of the Universe' and then gives a reason why that is so, connected to the matter in hand. So for the blessing before drinking wine we have 'who creates the fruit of the vine' and for the blessing of awaking we have 'who have, with compassion, returned my soul within me'. These prayers tend to focus on blessing God, through recognition and praise, rather than blessing in the sense of consecrating the thing that occasioned the prayer. Rabbi Meir recommended uttering 'a hundred benedictions' every day.[3]

We have surveyed some of the basic elements associated with blessing, and each of these has played some part in Christian life since the earliest times. For instance, we find a number of descriptions in the New Testament of people being set apart for various offices in the Church. We might think of the first seven deacons, with Stephen among their number, or of Timothy's appointment as a senior leader

---

2 See, for instance, *Hebrew Daily Prayer Book* (London: Collins, 2006), published by the United Synagogue, with a commentary by Sir Jonathan Sacks.

3 Quoted by Victor Gollancz, *The New Year of Grace: An Anthology for Youth and Age* (London: Gollancz, 1961), p. 62.

of the Church (1 Tim. 4.14). We might also consider marriage. While St Paul generally commends the unmarried state above the married one, he did not dishonour wedlock. Indeed, his argument for singleness – in the passage from 1 Corinthians 7 we discussed above – rests on the idea that the husband and wife are in some sense consecrated, or set apart, for each other, and Paul would prefer a single-hearted devotion to Christ (1 Cor. 7.32–34).[4] In the Letter to the Hebrews we also read of marriage as a sort of consecration: the 'marriage bed' is not to be 'defiled', and only that can be defiled which has first been set aside as holy (Heb. 13.4).

Moving beyond the New Testament, only fragments of the earliest Christian liturgies survive. From the second century we have evidence of a short service called the *lucernarium*, a service of blessing for newly kindled light, often associated with the evening meal. A hymn associated with this service – *Phos Hilaron* – was probably written around AD 300. It is still used in Orthodox worship to this day as well as in many other traditions, and might be familiar to some in translation as *Hail, Gladdening Light* or *O Gladsome Light*.

Hail, gladdening Light, of His pure glory poured
Who is the immortal Father, heavenly, blest,
Holiest of Holies – Jesus Christ our Lord!
Now we are come to the sun's hour of rest;
The lights of evening round us shine;
We hymn the Father, Son, and Holy Spirit divine!
Worthiest art thou at all times to be sung

---

4 I have discussed this passage, and related it to arguments in favour of marriage, in *Why Sacraments?* (London: SPCK/Eugene, OR: Wipf & Stock, 2013), pp. 116–17.

With undefiled tongue,
Son of our God, giver of life, alone:
Therefore in all the world thy glories, Lord, they own.[5]

From around the early third century we have the first complete example of a liturgy, preserved in the *Apostolic Tradition* of Hippolytus.[6] It includes fully written-out blessings for use in connection with various aspects of both everyday life and the life of the Church: blessings of milk, water, honey, new fruits and light, along with oil for the anointing of the sick. As far as we can see, these blessings were performed as part of the liturgy of the Eucharist. Occasional accounts of blessings outside the liturgy also come to us. St Anthony of Egypt (*c.* 251–356), for instance, was famed for his bestowal of protective blessings, as is recounted by St Athanasius (296/8–373) in his *Life of Anthony*.[7]

From the Middle Ages onwards we are provided with a wealth of liturgical texts from which to construct our history of blessing. The most significant documents are 'sacramentaries' – books that collated the prayers used to perform the various sacraments of the Church. Several different but connected traditions of sacramentary grew up, which preserve the liturgy used in a particular locality. The prayers in these collections are often both beautifully constructed and highly theological. The opening prayers they provide, on the theme of the day (called the 'collect'), are the source for those same

---

5 Translated by John Keble – see *Hymns Ancient and Modern Revised* (London: William Clowes & Sons, 1972).

6 The exact purpose of this text is unclear. It may be the order for an ordination rite rather than a usual Eucharist, and it may have served as an example rather than recording the actual practice of a particular local church. Its precise date is unknown. Some parts may be earlier than the early third century and some parts later.

7 Rivard, *Blessing the World*, p. 36.

prayers in several rites in our own time, including the liturgies of the Roman Catholic Church and the Church of England (in both the Book of Common Prayer and *Common Worship*).[8] We have most evidence for blessings performed within the setting of the Eucharist: the sacramentaries were, after all, by definition books for use in church services. We can, however, suppose that blessings were also performed in other situations. As Rivard puts it:

> Our comprehension of how the laity of the early Middle Ages understood these blessings is hampered by the lack of sources explicitly dealing with this form of ritual, which seems to have fallen into that rather paradoxical category of things so common as to be unworthy of mention.[9]

Since these sacramentaries have church liturgy in mind, we find particular attention to the blessing of things to be used in those services, such as oils for anointing and water for baptism, ash for Ash Wednesday, palms for Palm Sunday, the paschal candle for the Easter Vigil and food for Easter Day.[10] All of those objects or elements, and equivalent blessings, are in use today.

An important sacramentary, the 'Old Gelasian Sacramentary', is notable for containing blessings with a strong protective element.[11] Slightly later, with the Frankish-Gelasian

---

8 For a collection, see William Bright, *Ancient Collects and Other Prayers: Selected for Devotional Use from Various Rituals* (Oxford: Parker, 1862).

9 Rivard, *Blessing the World*, p. 34.

10 Rivard, *Blessing the World*, p. 30, quoting Pierre-Marie Gy, 'Benedictions', in Joseph R. Strayer (ed.), *Dictionary of the Middle Ages*, Vol. 2 (New York: Scribner, 1982–9), pp. 177–8, p. 177.

11 Rivard, *Blessing the World*, p. 31.

sacramentaries, such blessings as prayers for protection were cast even more strongly in terms of protection from evil powers. Gy suggests that this new prominence of prayers for protection against demonic forces may be a pastoral and missionary attempt to supplant traditional religions as Europe continued to be converted. These blessings are a Christian response to a perceived need, previously supplied by pagan religion and magic.[12] Whatever position we take about unseen powers, most Christians would say that the need for protection against evil is a real one and that the desire for this protection is a real and reasonable desire. The pagan response was illicit for Christians not because it was a response but because it was pagan.

Around the twelfth century, prayers and rites of blessing obtained their own separate volume, called a benedictional. Despite this change of anthologization, practices of blessing remained relatively unchanged into the middle of the twentieth century, at least in the Orthodox and Roman Catholic Churches. A significant date in the West was the publication of the Roman Ritual, or *Rituale Romanum*, by Pope Paul V in 1614, as part of the Counter- (or Catholic) Reformation. Like other aspects of this reform movement, the Ritual retained a strongly Catholic focus from previous centuries but sought for a leaner, streamlined piety. If elements of Christian practice were seen as potentially superstitious or not in keeping with Catholic doctrine, they were jettisoned, not least for the sake of making the Catholic faith more persuasive to newly arrived Protestants. (The exercise was fated to be only so effective: Protestant-minded Christians were bound to think that the Counter-Reformation soul-searching, when it came to 'superstition', did not go far

---

12 Gy, 'Benedictions', p. 177. Cited by Rivard, *Blessing the World*, p. 33.

enough.) Unlike other parts of the post-Tridentine reform, the Ritual was never imposed, and was intended to be a model to be adapted to local use.[13]

Over the course of successive editions, the Roman Ritual picked up a raft of additional, specific blessings, not least those associated with particular religious orders: Carmelites, Franciscans and so on.[14] Eventually the appendix became as long as the text behind which it sat. In the early to mid-twentieth century, the trend towards simplification resurfaced. Even more than before, anything that looked like 'folk religion' was frowned upon. These concerns were taken up as part of the reforms of the Second Vatican Council. This led to a general contraction of Catholic devotion: the previous tapestry of devotions to a wide variety of saints tended to be collapsed to very few – almost entirely the Blessed Virgin Mary, with perhaps some reference to St Joseph and St Peter; the liturgical life of the Church was reduced to the seven sacraments and the Divine Office. Piety at home concentrated on the rosary, with perhaps the occasional novena, a cycle of prayers over nine days. In a parallel fashion, blessings became less important in the life of the average catholic-minded Christian, and their justification tended to be worked out in terms of the sacraments. Consider Brian Magee's desire to understand blessings in relation to the sacraments, offered in his admirable introduction to *The Veritas Book of Blessing Prayers*: 'blessings . . . are prayers in praise of God which help to dispose the faithful for the fruitful use of the sacraments'.[15] This 'Vatican II trajectory' towards simplification found its

---

13 See Lang, 'Theologies of Blessing', p. 28.

14 It was expanded in 1874 and 1895.

15 Brian Magee, *The Veritas Book of Blessing Prayers* (Dublin: Veritas, 1989), p. 1.

culmination with the publication, in 1984,[16] of a rewritten *Book of Blessings*, which supplanted the Roman Ritual.[17]

In other words, there was a tendency from around the turn of the second half of the twentieth century to stress what blessings are not rather than what they are: that they are not sacraments and do not have the surety of sacraments. This sat alongside the tendency to 'purify' blessing rather than augment it, and to seek above all to guard against whatever might look like superstition or folk religion. As Patrick Bishop puts it in his article in the *New Dictionary of Sacramental Worship*, a later twentieth-century tendency among theorists of liturgy to stress that the *sacraments convey by themselves* the full meaning of encounter with Christ, 'has often been at the expense of the warmth of richness of Christian daily life'.[18] This in turn has tended towards a new emphasis on church-focused piety over domestic piety. This illustrates how reforms aimed at giving new prominence to the role of the laity can in fact serve to advance what might be called a 'clericalist' tendency.[19]

---

16 This is the date of the publication of the authoritative Latin text. Translations followed into vernacular languages.

17 In 2007, however, Pope Benedict XVI focused renewed attention on the 'Tridentine' rites put forward in the early seventeenth century with his Apostolic Letter *Summorum Pontificum*.

18 Patrick Bishop, 'Sacramentals', in P. E. Fink (ed.), *New Dictionary of Sacramental Worship* (Collegeville, MN: Liturgical Press, 1990), pp. 1114–15.

19 These perhaps unintended clericalist tendencies surface elsewhere in the liturgical reforms of the twentieth century. For instance, the orientation of the priest at the Eucharist was widely changed, from East (facing in the same direction as the people) to West (facing the people). This was intended to remove a purported sense of distance between the priest and the people. The effect, however, was to set the priest before the people head on, as a new focus of attention. To a new extent, the priest becomes a performer. The effect is even worse given the Vatican II tendency

The new *Book of Blessings* reflected contemporary thought on what it means to bless and was in turn influential on later thought and practice in Roman Catholic circles and beyond. The waning of widespread use of blessings, and of their riotous variety, was reflected in the prayers themselves, which are truncated compared to what had gone before and more uniform in structure. We might make a contrast with the prayers of the Roman Ritual. These had tended to be quite extended or to fall into many parts (such that, for instance, the blessing of water involves first the exorcism of the water, and of the salt that is to be added, alongside various other prayers), and to have a literary quality of layered references, often to scriptural texts. In contrast, the *Book of Blessings* has shorter, plainer prayers and anything that might look too eccentric – such as those exorcisms – was removed.

---

towards concelebration (celebration by more than one priest). The congregation is then faced with a whole *rank* of priests, who have their side of the altar (the 'business' side), which is not the people's side. Or consider the effect of the massive multiplication of choice among liturgical texts, of which the Church of England's *Common Worship* is a spectacular example. This choice is exercised by the priest or other minister, making him or her a 'liturgical technician'. While the earlier Book of Common Prayer was the common property of the whole of the Church of England, laity as much as clergy, the ten or more volumes of *Common Worship* are necessarily the preserve of the clergy alone. Before the liturgical reforms, the laity would be expected to own a Prayer Book and would be encouraged to understand it and memorize parts of it. In the present day, especially in the Church of England, there can be no expectation that the laity will own the complete *Common Worship* library. My grandmother, born in the early twentieth century, knew the rites of the Church from her childhood, and could meditate upon the services by which she would be confirmed, married and buried. No child born in the last 20 years could have any such expectation: the rites now belong to the clergy, those liturgical technicians, and are all but certain to have been rewritten in any case, perhaps more than once, by the time those events happen.

That gives something of the Roman Catholic trajectory. Retracing our course a little, back to the sixteenth century, the Reformation saw a far more radical curtailment of the practice of blessing in Protestant churches than would even be seen for Roman Catholics in the twentieth century. That said, we should note that those Protestant churches varied considerably from one another in this matter, as they still do: from Lutherans' greater tendency to preserve blessings to Zwinglians' greater tendency to suppress them, the Calvinists lying somewhere in between although probably nearer the Zwinglians.

The Church of England – and the other Anglican churches that proceeded from it – lives up to its characteristic position of standing between the Roman Catholic Church and the Protestant churches, although this story is not without twists and turns, and even lurches. We might take the example of a procession to bless fields just before Ascension, a period called 'Rogationtide' (see pp. 150–2). This thoroughly medieval practice was suppressed during the last year of the reign of Henry VIII but restored by Elizabeth I. It did not return with the full ceremonial of earlier times but we are left in no doubt that the restored rite seeks a blessing upon the earth. It represents an Anglican chastened Catholicism, but one not chastened enough for the growing Puritan wing of the Church. 'Popish' practices such as this were part of what led to the execution of Charles I, the Civil War and the Commonwealth. At the Restoration of the Crown and Episcopacy, just such practices were again raised as part of questions about the identity of the Established Church in England. Two sticking points for the Puritans – now politically defeated – bore upon elements of blessing, namely the use of the sign of the cross at baptism (it being the definitive sign, used down the Christian centuries, in the bestowal of a blessing) and the giving of a ring at marriage.[20] What blessing represents was very close to the nub of these arguments. Is salvation thoroughly material? Does it come to us through material means? Does the Church have the authority to proscribe certain rites and forms of prayer that, although contingent in themselves, take on a more binding character within that particular Christian community because the Church has promulgated them? The Church of England held to the ancient, Catholic understanding of these topics, found right back in the earliest Fathers. Many Puritan ministers at the time found this too much to stomach. They would not promise their obedience in these matters and had to leave the Church of England.

Blessings remained, in their low-key way, in the liturgy of the Prayer Book through to the present day.[21] The Oxford Movement in the nineteenth century opened the way to some appropriation of traditions from the wider Western Church. The liturgical revisions of the twentieth century formalized this, giving the Church of England a wider and wider official range of prayers and rites of blessing.

---

20 The ring was not likely to be blessed but its status as an *object* brought into the liturgy of the Church bears directly on the question of whether we embrace or flee from materiality.

21 While not exactly a blessing, attention might be paid to the service entitled 'The Thanksgiving of Woman after Child-Birth, Commonly Called the Churching of Woman'. The element of recognition and thanksgiving is particularly prominent. The service has come to be treated with scorn by some liturgical commentators because of associations with 'purification', as though childbirth was somehow defiling and this service was required to restore the woman to a state of purity. The words of the service itself do not bear out that interpretation. It is a simple act of thanksgiving.

A similar story could be told for other churches. In the chapters that follow in this second part of the book, we will consider some of the ways the practice of blessing might become an even more prominent part of the life of Christians, both individually and as local communities.

11

Who and What is Blessed?

At the heart of the Church's ministry of blessing is the blessing of people. What they are blessed to do or be will differ, to some extent, from age to age. The early Church, for instance, had a recognized office of the widow, who had dedicated her widowhood to God. Today we find few consecrated widows. Other offices were retained for longer and then lost, or lost and revived – such as the doorkeeper (now more or less forgotten in most rites) and the reader (lost in the Roman Catholic Church, and in the Church of England, but revived in the latter in 1886).

In practice the various answers to the question posed by the title of this chapter turn out to be less distinct than we might think, whether we answer 'people', 'things', 'places' or 'actions'. The blessing of light, which we have already encountered, hovers between the blessing of an object (the light), of an action (lighting the lamp) and of a time (the dusk). If we bless someone's Lenten intention we are blessing both a person and an endeavour and, in a way, a time: the Lenten fast. In this chapter we will concentrate on some of the less obvious recipients of blessing: places, relationships and actions or endeavours.

Blessing Places

By blessing places we acknowledge the significance of *place* for human beings in general and for many aspects of human life in particular. If a place is going to be important for us then it is natural that a Christian would want it to be important in a way that recognizes, thanks, praises and invokes God; that is, to bring to the place all the elements associated with the act of blessing. Blessing might come particularly naturally for those places that are bound up with central features of blessing in general, namely the flourishing of human life in fruitfulness of all kinds. We see that with houses, and we see it also with two of the other principal locations for geographical blessings, namely the fields in which we grow crops and graze animals and, less prominently, seas and rivers, which in their own way contribute to human fruitfulness and flourishing, either through fish or as routes for commerce. We will return to the blessing of houses and of fields below, in Chapter 14 on when to bless.

A word might be in order about both of these sorts of blessings. Records suggest that, since the fifth century, prayers for the fruitfulness of the fields – with fasting – have been offered by Christians in the days before the Feast of the Ascension. Spring was under way and the growth towards harvest was in God's hands. Over time this ceremony became associated with the Sunday after the Ascension. The Gospel reading for that Sunday was from John 16 (and still is in some rites), which promises that what the disciples ask in the name of Christ, they will receive, and one of the Latin verbs for 'to ask' is *rogare*, which is the origin of 'Rogation Sunday' and 'Rogationtide'. For a community that lived from year to year on the produce of the fields, little would come more naturally, given such an invitation, than to ask for a blessing upon crops and cattle. If our immediate impulse is different, that only serves to show how anomalous our position is relative to all of the rest of history – an anomaly also expressed in the unfamiliarity of a new generation with the basics of the production of food. If the blessing of fields – and seas and rivers – served to put people back in touch with the environment, that would be no bad thing, and might be part of encouraging a more ethical relation to the rest of creation.

This yearly observance took the form of 'beating the bounds' – which is to say, of a procession around the boundary of the particular parish, reciting a litany, singing psalms and stopping for prayers and blessings at various parts. One parish I know in Cambridge makes a not-at-all-facetious use of Psalm 36, with its apposite line 'Thou, LORD, shalt save both man and beast; How excellent is thy mercy, O God : and the children of men shall put their trust under the shadow of thy wings.'[1]

Rogation processions were suppressed in the last year of the reign of Henry VIII but were restored by Elizabeth I. The form of service makes it clear that this was seen as a revival of the practice of blessing the fields. The priest and poet George Herbert wrote about Rogation processions in *The Country Parson*:

The Country Parson is a lover of old customs, if they be good . . . Particularly, he loves procession, and maintains it, because there are contained therein four manifest advantages: first, a blessing of God for the fruits of the field; secondly, justice in the preservation of bounds; thirdly, charity in loving walking, and neighbourly accompanying one another, with reconciling of

---

1 In Coverdale's translation from the Book of Common Prayer.

differences at that time, if there be any; fourthly, mercy in relieving the poor by a liberal distribution and largesse, which at that time is, or ought to be used. Wherefore he exacts of all to be present at the perambulation.[2]

Today this practice is continued in some Anglican parishes, predominantly rural ones. It provides a good way for the Church to make herself visible outside of church buildings. Since the early twentieth century, harvest festival services have become popular as another service associated with the provision of the earth. (Many people are surprised by the relatively recent arrival of this service as a fixture in the calendar, although there are ancient precedents, suppressed at the Reformation. See also the discussion of Lammastide and harvest festival below, pp. 198–200.) Rogationtide focuses on blessing as invocation, and harvest festival – and its ancient precursors – on blessing as praise and thanksgiving.

Terra firma is not the only such setting. Christian places and cultures with a maritime tradition have often blessed seas and rivers. As an example, to this day clergy and people from the two Anglican dioceses in London – Southwark, south of the River Thames, and London, north of it – meet in the middle of London Bridge each year on the Feast of the Baptism of Christ, to pronounce together a blessing upon the river that so defines the city and was once the principal artery of its commerce.

---

2 George Herbert, *The Country Parson*, Ch. 35, spelling and punctuation modernized. We might note the significance of maintaining boundaries of land justly, a concern expressed in the Old Testament (e.g. Prov. 22.28; Deut. 19.14; 27.17) and taken up in the Church of England's 'Commination' Service, which contained the following line among its various responses: '*Minister*: Cursed is he that removeth his neighbour's landmark. *Answer* [by the assembled congregation]: Amen.'

The concept of blessing is close to the concept of dedication, which is to say, of setting some place (or thing or person) aside for a certain (or 'dedicated') task. The blessing of a home is an example of this but so is the consecration of a burial ground. The more highly charged and significant the purpose, the more likely we are to want such a dedication. The burial ground is a good example since the burial of the dead is of the highest significance and the ground that receives the remains of the dead comes to bear a highly charged emotional character. There is something primordial about this urge; it comes entirely naturally. It is the context, for instance, of Abraham Lincoln's famous Gettysburg Address (of 'government of the people, by the people, for the people'):[3]

> We are met on a great battle-field . . . We have come to dedicate a portion of that field, as a final resting place for those who here gave their lives that that nation might live. It is altogether fitting and proper that we should do this. But, in a larger sense, we can not dedicate – we can not consecrate – we can not hallow – this ground. The brave men, living and dead, who struggled here, have consecrated it, far above our poor power to add or detract.

Lincoln reminds us that dedicating a portion of a field is natural; it is 'altogether fitting and proper'. He also remind us that places acquire a character, meaning and resonance whether we like it or not; the battle has already left its spiritual mark on the terrain. The religious impulse to bless

---

3 Of 19 November, 1863.

places acknowledges this and seeks to channel it aright, to enhance the good and restrain the ill.[4]

Some churches still bless fields or graveyards, many will bless houses, but almost all will have some sort of blessing or consecration of a new church building. While this may not happen often, blessing is more or less ubiquitous when it does. The blessing of church buildings used to be an elaborate process. In keeping with current liturgical tastes, it is likely to be less elaborate today. All the same, it may still involve prayers at different parts (or 'stations') of the building, and not only a great deal of sprinkling with holy water but also signing the walls in various places with holy oil (the 'oil of chrism', otherwise used at a baptism, confirmation, ordination or coronation). These sites of anointing are sometimes marked out with crosses carved into the walls, as a reminder of the day of dedication. If so, a good visual reminder at the yearly anniversary of this event can be to burn a candle in front of the mark.

Blessing places may come naturally, and blessing a church building might seem particularly obvious, but it is also a matter of perplexity for some Christians, who may wonder why we dedicate particular places for the worship of God when God is everywhere present. Indeed, they might wonder why we go to the trouble of even building churches. One answer would be that the business of worship is not in fact like other human activities, and for that reason we might usefully have buildings that are rather unlike other buildings. Worship transcends distinctions of time and place, joining us with people of every place and

---

4 As a parallel example we have from the Old Testament the idea of intentional desecration: that the way to deal with the dedication of a place to a foreign god was to scatter the ashes of the dead, so as to destroy its sense of consecration to an alien religion (see 2 Kings 23.16).

age. By its architecture and quality of execution, a church building stands as a sort of perpetual offering.

As for the idea that buildings are unnecessary, it is certainly the case that God can and ought to be praised 'always and everywhere', as a Eucharistic Prayer has it. There is a universality here that is grounded in the simplicity and transcendence of God. All the same, human worship is necessarily human and, unlike God, we are not simple or transcendent; we are not present in all times and places like God is. The human being is finite and particular, and human worship will therefore have this character. A supreme writer on this territory was G. K. Chesterton. People have always, he wrote, pursued a particular course when it comes to holiness: 'they have marked it out in particular spaces', just as they have, for instance, differentiated between days in their religious calendars. He called this the 'chivalry and dignity of definition', over and against 'the degradation of infinity'.[5] He saw here a universal principle which, while ancient, was confirmed by the incarnation. The shepherds of Bethlehem travelled to the manger, to a particular place, and there they 'found their Shepherd'. This act of journeying was validated by the arrival of the Christ Child. In Chesterton's words:

> the population had been wrong in many things; but they had not been wrong in believing that holy things could have a habitation and that divinity need not distain the limits of time and space.[6]

---

5 G. K. Chesterton, 'The Philosophy of Islands', published in *The Venture: An Annual of Art and Literature* (London: John Baillie, 1903), pp. 2–9, p. 8. Collected in Dorothy Collins (ed.), *The Spice of Life, and Other Essays* (Bakersfield, IA: Darwen Finlayson, 1964).

6 G. K. Chesterton, *The Everlasting Man* (San Francisco: Ignatius Press, 1993), p. 174.

Alongside all the sorts of theological arguments that could be advanced for the building and consecration of churches[7] stand practical ones, although the two are related. Setting aside a place for God means that there is a place for people to seek God when they want to seek him. We are bodily creatures, and while anyone can journey into the interior distances of their soul, they might also find it helpful to travel some physical distance. Pilgrimage sites remain as popular as ever, at least in the UK – perhaps more popular than they have been for decades, whether that is the Shrine of Our Lady of Walsingham or Holy Trinity Brompton. Pope Francis commented on this in his first apostolic exhortation, *Evangelii Gaudium*, calling upon Christians everywhere to leave the doors of their churches open so that people would have places to seek and encounter God.

> A Church which 'goes forth' is a Church whose doors are open . . . At times we have to be like the father of the prodigal son, who always keeps his door open so that when the son returns, he can readily pass through it. The Church is called to be the house of the Father, with doors always wide open. One concrete sign of such openness is that our church doors should always be open, so that if someone, moved by the Spirit, comes there looking for God, he or she will not find a closed door . . . the Church is not a tollhouse; it is the house of the Father, where there is a place for everyone, with all their problems.[8]

Before we can leave our church doors open (which is not always an easy task), we need churches with doors to open.

---

7 See, for instance, Andrew Davison and Alison Milbank, *For the Parish: A Critique of Fresh Expressions* (London: SCM Press, 2010), pp. 144–69.

8 *Evangelii Gaudium*, §§46–7.

Blessing Actions and Endeavours

The blessing of light, which we have already covered, was an important blessing in the early Church, observed with its hymn *Phos Hilaron* ('Hail, Gladdening Light'). We find a blessing at the lighting of the lamps very much later, and a long way away, in the seventeenth-century world of – once again – George Herbert. As he writes in *The Country Parson*:

> Another old custom there is of saying, when light is brought in, God send us the light of heaven; and the Parson likes this very well; neither is he afraid of praising, or praying to God at all times, but is rather glad of catching opportunities to do them. Light is a great blessing, and as great as food, for which we give thanks: and those that think this superstitious, neither know superstition, nor themselves.[9]

Herbert mentions two activities here that can call for blessing: lighting of the lamps and gathering for a meal. The advent of electricity probably makes the first less notable, although the drawing in of darkness remains a reasonable event in the day to mark with a prayer. The blessing of food, however, remains an obvious and worthy daily occasion for prayer. So do journeys.

The *Rule of Saint Benedict*, the model for Western monasticism, stipulates: 'Let brethren who are to be sent on a journey commend themselves to the prayers of all the brethren and to the abbot.' This chapter of the *Rule* goes on: 'and always at the last prayer of the Office let there be a commemoration of all absent brethren.'

---

9 Herbert, *Country Parson*, Ch. 35, spelling and capitalization modernized.

From this monastic tradition has come down to us a set of prayers for the blessing of a journey known as the *Itinerarium*. It is provided in some books of blessings, and a simple online search will bring up several versions and translations. Traditionally it is built around the Benedictus (the Song of Zechariah from Luke's Gospel), with its line about 'guiding our feet into the way of peace'. That canticle is sandwiched between a prayer, said before and after it (the 'antiphon'), asking for the guidance of the angels, followed by a set of responses drawn from scriptural texts with a journeying theme, and concluding with several prayers (of 'collect' form), some of them as old as the eighth century. It is a beautiful form of prayer and deserves to be better known.

In the cycle of the year, we might think of two periods when we bless endeavours in the form of a good 'intention', namely blessing of New Year's and Lenten resolutions. When I was at university, the chaplain of my college used to put on a pre-Lent service each year, loosely inspired by the Eastern Orthodox observance of 'Forgiveness Sunday', a day in the year when the members of a congregation seek one another out to ask for, and offer, forgiveness where it is necessary. The structure of the service was much as might be expected, being arranged as a sequence of Bible readings, prayers and hymns. There was, however, a period of unstructured time towards the end, when that reconciliation could be sought. During that period the chaplain would sit up by the altar and we could go to commit ourselves to some Lenten resolution or other, and receive his blessing. This model, in several of its aspects, strikes me as a good one.

The opportunities for blessing endeavours and activities are more or less endless. Some have prayers or blessings of long standing associated with them, such as 'vestry prayers' for before and after conducting divine service, or a prayer attributed to Thomas Aquinas for use before study. The Eastern Orthodox tradition even provides a few prayers for use before *any* action, should a more specific prayer be lacking. Here are two:

> Lord Jesus Christ, my God, you have said, 'Apart from me, you can do nothing.' In faith I embrace your words, Lord, and I entreat your goodness. Help me to carry out the work I am about to begin, and to bring it to completion. To you I give glory, Father, Son and Holy Spirit. Amen.

> My Lord and Saviour, you became a human being and laboured with your hands until the time of your ministry began. Bless me as I begin this work and help me to bring it to completion. Lord, enlighten my mind and strengthen my body, that I may accomplish my task according to your will. Guide me to bring about works of goodness to your service and glory. Amen.[10]

Refusing to Bless

Some contemporary prayers do not – quite – bless because of either a certain failure of nerve about the business of blessing or some misguided theology. That observation, however, does not exhaust the field of 'not blessing'. Any consideration of the subject of blessing should include some thought about what we, quite categorically, do not bless.

---

10 As given, for instance, at www.orthodoxprayer.org/OtherPrayers. html, accessed 10 January 2014; here adapted.

We can start with a comment from the Second Vatican Council: 'There is scarcely any proper use of material things which cannot be thus directed toward the sanctification of men and the praise of God.'[11] This gives us three angles on what we might choose not to bless: that which is not a proper use of a material thing, that which stands against human sanctification and that which contradicts or impedes the praise of God. Christianity is not alone in holding to such strictures: there are no Jewish blessings for either forbidden foods or forbidden activities.

That could be said to be that. We should not bless that which is improper, unholy or impious, and it lies beyond the scope of this book to set out in any comprehensive way the principles upon which we could judge those criteria. One useful approach, however, might be made through the link between blessing and eschatology: blessings serving the purpose of aligning things with their destiny in the redeemed kingdom of God. What, we can therefore ask, makes for an anticipation of the life of the world to come? This proves to be a good justification for not blessing weapons, something that is specifically forbidden in the Roman Catholic Church, since the eschatological vision is a world without weapons: swords are beaten into ploughshares (Isa. 2.4).[12] Similarly, the Catholic prohibition of blessing political emblems[13] can be seen as expressing a desire to see beyond the political divisions they represent in light of the unity of the kingdom of God.

---

11 *Sacrosanctum Concilium*, §61.

12 The blessing of weapons and warriors had become common in the Latin West by the tenth century – Lawrence G. Duggan, *Armsbearing and the Clergy in the History and Canon Law of Western Christianity* (Woodbridge: The Boydell Press, 2013), p. 109. On it now being forbidden in the Roman Catholic Church, see Herbert Vorgrimler, *Sacramental Theology* (Collegeville, MN: Liturgical Press, 1992), p. 317.

13 Vorgrimler, *Sacramental Theology*, p. 317.

Blessing Relationships

For many Christians today, the sharpest question when it comes to what to bless – or not to bless – is likely to concern same-sex relationships. The situation is evolving quickly, not least in the UK, so it would be foolish to comment on it with too much specificity. The reader's mind, in any case, will be strongly informed by his or her own ethical perspective on this question, and the ethical question is prior to the liturgical one: what we bless is determined by what we think is good. That said, the connection between blessing and ethics is so strong that the theological perspectives obtained from our discussion of blessing can provide some helpful angles for thinking about the ethical question.

Blessings, for instance, both recognize a relation between what we bless and the hope for the life of the world, and further cement it. We can therefore usefully ask whether same-sex relationships embody something of that eschatological hope, either in general or in a particular case before us. Do they, for instance, or does it, represent something of how we expect the life of the world to come to look? Are the virtues that remain into the next age – faith, hope and love (1 Cor. 13.13) – nurtured by the relationship in question? Do we see what flows from love, the supreme virtue among those three, which 'never ends' (1 Cor. 13.8): patience and kindness, the cessation of envy, boastfulness, arrogance and rudeness, and growing beyond insistence on one's own way, irritability and resentfulness – and so on (1 Cor. 13.4–7)?

Other categories from earlier in this book will offer additional avenues down which to approach the underlying ethical question. Is the relationship an occasion for thanksgiving to God, for instance? Does it appear to us, and to the couple, as a matter of vocation, both filling out their humanity and demanding an element of consecration, not least in 'forsaking all others'?

In asking such questions, we are not judging whether a relationship is *perfect*. Few heterosexual relationships, after all, are entirely uncomplicated. When we bless any relationship we acknowledge both what is good and what is in need of redemption and ongoing attention. Blessing, as we noted in Chapter 2, involves both 'thanksgiving' and 'beseeching'.[14] The terms are Gordon Lathrop's, and he has himself brought them to bear upon this particular question. His conclusion is worth quoting in full:

> If our culture is beginning to explore the social impor-
> tance of faithful gay and lesbian relationships, and, what
> is more, if baptized Christians are experiencing the good-
> ness of God in these relationships, prayers that give thanks
> for God's goodness, remember Jesus Christ, and beseech
> God's Spirit in such relationships – that they may be hospi-
> table and caring in a needy and lonely world – are certainly
> called for. So are the old critical questions that correspond
> to the beseechings. Here might be some such questions:
> Have you freely agreed to do this? Are you promising life-
> long fidelity? Will your fidelity be marked out not only by
> sexual monogamy but also by care for the other? Will your
> hearth be a place of hospitality? In a church more cen-
> tred on eucharist and more prodigal with all of its prayers
> of blessing, such a prayer might be no big thing . . . And
> thanksgiving and beseeching are, together, not just a pat-
> tern of prayer but a way that a Christian in any cultural
> arrangement may live with the mystery of sex.[15]

---

14 Gordon Lathrop, *Holy Ground: A Liturgical Cosmology* (Minneapolis, MN: Fortress Press, 2003), p. 85.

15 Lathrop, *Holy Ground*, pp. 87–8.

Among the themes explored in this book we might consider one more, which is the category of life and abundance. We could scarcely find a better topic for the sort of honest and courageous conversations that are needed across the battle lines drawn up over this subject. Those who wish to celebrate same-sex relationships will, likely as not, take it as obvious and central to the discussion that these sexual relationships, between people who are committed and well suited to each other, are a matter of life and abundance. On the other hand, those who cannot accept such relationships, also on theological grounds, are equally likely to take it as obvious and central to the discussion that these relationships are fundamentally opposed to life and abundance.

Any attempt to address this question will benefit from an empirical dimension: the question as to whether a relationship leads to life and fulfilment of life is something relatively open to observation. That said, there is obviously also theological material that demands to be taken into consideration, and the opening chapters of Genesis will be one of the most significant sources. From Genesis 2 we see the importance of companionship to human flourishing, not least with the comment that it is not good for the man to be alone (Gen. 2.18). Companionship is perhaps the most valuable blessing that we are afforded as human beings.[16] Even closer to the beginning, in Genesis 1, we encounter the primordial pronouncement of blessing on the human race:

---

16 Some Christians place particular emphasis on the fact that Adam is presented with a female partner with whom not to be alone. We should also note, however, that Adam does not in the first instance celebrate the *difference* of Eve but her similarity to him: that she is another human being is more important than her gender at this instance: 'This at last is bone of my bones and flesh of my flesh' (Gen 2.23).

God blessed them, and God said to them, 'Be fruitful and multiply, and fill the earth and subdue it; and have dominion over the fish of the sea and over the birds of the air and over every living thing that moves upon the earth.' (Gen. 1.28)

Again, this passage will constitute something of a battle-ground for arguments about the legitimacy of same-sex relationships. The foregoing discussions in this book will have shown that it does not bear unequivocally against valuing them. The biblical and wider theological traditions, for instance, urge us to see this call to fruitfulness and multiplication as extending beyond physical childbirth, while still very much valuing that dimension of human life.

In the New Testament any sense that human blessedness is irrevocably bound up with childbearing is radically subverted in the person of Christ himself. He was the perfectly blessed human being and he gathered a family to himself not by natural birth but by winning brothers and sisters through his death and resurrection, making him 'the first-born within a large family' (Rom. 8.29).[17] We also see this subversion in the many other passages that dethrone marriage and childbearing from the centre of human fulfilment (passages that the later theological tradition was generally at pains to show did not, however, undermine the value of human parenthood). We have considered his call to leave 'house or brothers or sisters or mother or father or children or fields' (Mark 10.28–30), and there are many others.[18]

---

17 See also Colossians 1.18.

18 Examples would include Matthew 8.21–22; 10.35–37 (and parallel in Luke); 12.46–50 (and parallels); Luke 11.27–28; 14.26; John 19.25–27. More gently, we see something of this shift in the development from polygamy to monogamy across the story of the Scriptures: the depth

While this expansion of our sense of human fruitfulness and abundance is primarily a New Testament development, we already have a sense of it in the blessing of Abraham. This begins 'I will make your offspring as numerous as the stars of heaven and as the sand that is on the seashore' (Gen. 22.17) but also includes the promise that 'by your offspring shall all the nations of the earth gain blessing for themselves' (Gen. 22.18): the blessing of abundance and fruitfulness that Abraham receives stretches beyond physical offspring. By definition, those other 'nations' are not his physical descendants.

This broader sense of where the blessedness of human fruitfulness lies finds good theological parallels in theological meditations on the 'good of marriage' – traditionally one of three – called 'offspring'. Thomas Aquinas, for instance, wrote that we cannot simply see this 'good' as exhausted in bearing additional children for the human family. It has a wider context, which he took to be 'the partnership of a common life, whereby each one contributes his share of work to the common stock'.[19] When we say that a marriage should include 'offspring', that means:

> not only the begetting of children, but also their education, which is the goal to which the whole endeavour of shared works of the husband and wife is directed, since parents naturally 'lay up' for their 'children' (2 Cor. 12.14).[20]

---

of a relationship with a single wife is more important than the abundance of children that might come from having many wives.

19 *ST Supplement* 49.2, *obj.* 1, citing Aristotle, *Nicomachean Ethics* VIII.12.

20 *ST Supplement* 49.2 ad 1.

Many same-sex relationships today do involve bringing up children, either because they have been adopted or are the natural offspring of one partner and not the other. Even when they do not, however, these couples often take an exemplary part in the 'shared work' of the community (as I have noted elsewhere),[21] to which this good of marriage belongs: in relation to the care and education of children, certainly, but in other ways also. This 'good of marriage' naturally takes on the wider 'outward-facing' dimensions to a marriage and indeed a heterosexual marriage that failed to contribute to the overall nurture of the wider community would be a deficient one, even if there were children. Every married couple is called to be a blessing to the wider community in this way, whether or not they have, or are capably of having, children of their own.

These are some of the considerations that the subject of blessing throws up for any consideration of the ethics of same-sex marriages. There would be others. The implication is not that the decision to bless precedes the adjudication as to what is good, but rather that the closeness of the association between blessing and celebration means that the criteria for what we mean by blessing help us to assess what we can and cannot celebrate.

---

21 *Why Sacraments?* (London: SPCK/Eugene, OR: Wipf & Stock, 2013), p. 119.

12

Who Blesses?

Blessing is a priestly action, which is not to say that it is an activity restricted to those who have received the office of priest or bishop through ordination. Blessing is a priestly activity, but Christ's people are a priestly people – not some only, but all of them. The Church is, as we read in 1 Peter 2.9, a 'royal priesthood'. With this in mind we can explore the ways in which pronouncing a blessing can, and perhaps should, feature in the life of those lay members who are the vast majority of the Church.

The *Catechism of the Catholic Church* helpfully maintains that 'every baptized person is called to be a "blessing", and to bless'.[1] On account of that, lay people 'may preside at certain blessings' but 'the more a blessing concerns ecclesial and sacramental life, the more is its administration reserved to the ordained ministry (bishops, priests, or deacons)'.[2]

We will turn to that question shortly. First, it is important to note how mistaken it would be to attend to blessing as a lay work as if this were solely a question of whether lay people can pronounce a liturgical or quasi-liturgical blessing.

---

1 *Catechism of the Catholic Church* (London: Burns & Oates, 2004; see also www.vatican.va/archive/ENG0015/_INDEX.HTM), §1669, citing Genesis 12.2; Luke 6.28; Romans 12.14; 1 Peter 3.9.

2 *Catechism of the Catholic Church*, §1669, citing *Sacrosanctum Concilium*, 79; *Code of Canon Law*, canon 1168; *De Benedictionibus*, 16, 18.

This would ignore much that is important about the lay vocation and, for that matter, much of what blessing means (important and valid though this solemn pronouncing of blessing certainly is).

Alison Milbank has written on this topic, and she observes two sides to the development of our sense of lay participation in liturgy. On the one hand, a restored sense of lay participation in the Eucharist has been an important and welcome development in recent decades. The Eucharist – that supreme act of blessing – is not the work of the priest in any sense that excludes it from being the work of the whole people of God. 'Liturgy', after all, derives from the Greek *laos* ('people') and *ergon* ('work' – as in 'urge'): it is a public work or duty. On the other hand, we should not so 'clericalize' our sense of lay participation as to forget, as Milbank puts it, that there is a 'priesthood of the laity in the secular world', a 'specific mission [which] is [often] forgotten and unresourced'.[3]

This mission of each Christian is undertaken in the situations in which they find themselves, which for most people will be their 'occupation' – the paternal and maternal realm of the home being very much part of what is meant here. In each situation or occupation our work of mission is not simply a matter of 'testimony' – for all Milbank, and I, would see that as important. Or if we *are* to characterize it as testimony through and through, then that will be because we have come to understand 'testimony' as running further than only and simply a *verbal* witness to Christ. Christians in their workplaces, as Milbank puts it, are 'already testifying by the way they handle the money, fill in the forms, bathe the children or treat the customers'.[4]

---

3 Andrew Davison and Alison Milbank, *For the Parish: A Critique of Fresh Expressions* (London: SCM Press, 2010), p. 134.

4 Davison and Milbank, *For the Parish*, p. 135.

She rightly calls this 'priestly' work. It is part of how the work of all Christians is one of blessing: 'it is transformative in taking the matter of the world and making it into praise, and restoring it to order and connection with God and humanity.'[5] Here we see those two counterpoised elements of blessing – of celebration and redemption – expressed in the way that any and every Christian is called to work: on the one hand, 'revealing what is good, true and beautiful' about the work we do, and on the other, going about it in such a way as to exercise judgement concerning 'their negative and destructive features'.[6] Milbank ties this back to the eucharistic theme, which is properly pervasive in discussions of blessing:

> Most trades have the potential to be transformative: to be eucharistic in giving meaning and value to the matter with which they deal. Helping people to understand how they may already be participating in God's mission by the way they handle the guy-ropes or treat their clients is part of the mission of the Church.[7]

For most of Christian history it has been natural both to see these activities themselves as acts of blessing and to ally them with specific pronouncements or invocations of blessing so as to recognize this. The work of the farmer is a blessing to the community, and this is taken up into blessings of the fields, perhaps on Rogation Sunday. Such associations between activity and prayer are bound to spring up. We prepare food for ourselves and for others, entering into the business of blessing by our actions, and we say grace; we build houses and we bless them; we bury the dead with dignity and we bless graves.

---

5 Davison and Milbank, *For the Parish*, p. 135.
6 Davison and Milbank, *For the Parish*, p. 136.
7 Davison and Milbank, *For the Parish*, p. 136.

There is a blessing that is about labour and a blessing that is liturgical. The two co-inhere, and if one aspect seems to bring the theological aspect more prominently to the fore (in the saying of grace, for example), in another sense the other, more practical aspect is primary, in the very obvious sense that if no one had cooked a meal there would be nothing to bless. George Herbert also let the everyday custom of blessing ground the more heightened liturgical forms: 'if all men are to bless upon occasion, as appears (Rom. 12.14), how much more those who are spiritual Fathers?'[8]

I hope that readers of this book will find some encouragement here to observe the liturgical and prayerful form of blessing, which could find expression in grace before meals, recitation of Thomas Aquinas's prayer before study or of the Eastern Orthodox 'Prayer before any Activity', or in any other of the blessings discussed in this second portion of the book. There would be something perverse, however, if recovery of the liturgical act of blessing were seen as an end in itself, deflecting our attention from seeing the business of everyday life as a blessing and an opportunity to bless – a participation, that is, in the work of God by which we are blessed, as are our communities.

Claus Westermann wisely pointed out that blessing relates profoundly to the well-being of the community and its prosperity (provided we have a purified and enlarged sense of what prosperity might amount to).[9] This itself suggests that blessing is profoundly a lay task. Gérard Philips noticed this, writing on lay vocation in 1956. A central component of the calling of every Christian, he wrote, is

---

8 George Herbert, *The Country Parson*, Ch. 36.

9 Claus Westermann, *Blessing in the Bible and the Life of the Church* (Philadelphia, PA: Fortress Press, 1978; first published in German in 1968), pp. 32–4.

'work for the prosperity of the community' – as much for the lay Christian as the cleric. This, alongside 'self-sacrifice for their families' (which carries a clear note of consecration), is nothing less than a 'sacred obligation'.[10]

As Philips put it, addressing in the first place his fellow Roman Catholics:

The lay Catholic is the one to assume the task of constructing the temporal city attached, in its way, to the city of God . . . They refuse idolatrous worship of the State but they do not refuse to serve. This is specifically lay territory; it is theirs to be engaged here wholeheartedly and to make the Gospel spirit felt.[11]

The Earth, as he put it, is not 'a definitive dwelling place' and 'still less . . . an imaginary paradise', but that should not deflect us from working to make it 'habitable'.[12] As Dominikus Thalhammer put it, central to the lay vocation is the work of bringing to 'perfection' that 'bit of the order of creation to which it [the particular lay vocation] pertains according to the laws inscribed in it by God'.[13] This is the commission (marked by greatness, as Thalhammer puts it), whereby we 'serve Christ as an instrument in the sanctification and transformation of the Cosmos'. By our work, our task is 'to carry, as it were, the incarnation of the Word into the heart of the Cosmos'.[14]

---

10 Gérard Philips, *The Role of the Laity in the Church* (Chicago: Fides, 1956), trans. John R. Gilbert, p. 150. This and the following quotations from Philips are suggested in John D. Gerken, *Toward a Theology of the Layman* (New York: Herder & Herder, 1963).

11 Philips, *Role of the Laity*, p. 51.

12 Philips, *Role of the Laity*, p. 46.

13 Dominikus Thalhammer, quoted by Gerken, *Toward a Theology of the Layman*, p. 99.

14 Thalhammer in Gerken, *Toward a Theology of the Layman*, p. 99.

By all means, then, let us explore the possibility for liturgical blessings in the life of lay Christians, but let it not deflect us from seeing the lay vocation as one of blessing, through and through, by which the world is sanctified, God is honoured, needs are relieved and the human community is made to flourish.

Blessing by Deacons

In earlier centuries, blessing was reserved to priests and bishops rather than deacons, and that remains the general rule today. Contemporary Roman Catholic practice, at least as expressed in the *Code of Canon Law* of 1983, envisages bishops and priests as the usual ministers of blessings,[15] and deacons as exercising only a more limited, delegated role.[16] The priest's authority to bless is itself delegated, and is received at ordination from the bishop as a delegated share of episcopal authority and ministry. Here, however, the priest's ministry of blessing is seen as so much part of the priesthood per se that the presumption is of an authority to bless. It is restricted only in view of instances of blessing that properly belong to the bishop (such as consecrating churches) or because something is, in itself, unworthy of blessing (such as armaments). The situation with the deacon is rather the other way around. Blessing is not primarily a diaconal role but some specific and limited dispensations to bless may, from time to time, be given by an explicit episcopal mandate.

---

15 'Any presbyter can impart blessings except those reserved to the Roman Pontiff or bishops' (canon 1169.2).

16 'A deacon can impart only those blessings expressly permitted by law' (canon 1169.3).

In theory, in the Roman Catholic Church a deacon can bless only in one of a certain number of enumerated circumstances.[17] In practice a more general 'rule of thumb' is likely to be employed, such as that deacons can perform short blessings of devotional items or more involved blessings when a priest is not present. Certainly some blessings are inherently priestly because they fall to the celebrant of a Eucharist, such as the blessing of ash on Ash Wednesday or of palms on Palm Sunday. The Church of England generally does not rule on this sort of question, but we can note that blessing is described as a priestly task in the ordinal. An annex to the canons, published by the two archbishops, dispenses deacons to bless the rings and the couple at a wedding, while adding that having weddings conducted by a deacon will be an unusual exception to general practice, perhaps because the couple is well known to the deacon in question. In that circumstance, however, a priest, if present, should bless the congregation as a whole at the end of the service. The logic seems to be that an exception is being made for the deacon to conduct the marriage, again perhaps because he or she knows the couple, but that the exception need not, and therefore should not, apply to addressing the congregation as a whole. We might also note that the Church of England expects this general blessing upon the people to be conducted by a bishop, if a bishop is present (as also the absolution).[18]

---

17 See Uwe Michael Lang, 'Theologies of Blessing: Origins and Characteristics of *De benedictionibus* (1984)', *Antiphon* 15.1 (2011), pp. 38, 40–2.

18 This is spelt out in the Book of Common Prayer in more than one place, for instance. A distinction might perhaps be observed between a bishop being present *as a bishop*, as part of the service, and a bishop happening to be in the building. It is not clear that a bishop on a rare Sunday off, sitting in the back of a congregation, is to be called upon to step in at these two points.

'Reserved' Blessings

Before the reforms of the Second Vatican Council, a broad range of blessings were said to be 'reserved' to certain traditions, at least in the Roman Catholic Church, as a sort of privilege. If a particular devotion had grown up within a certain tradition, then a degree of continuing association remained, although there was a desire not to suggest that any particular approach to prayer was 'owned' by any particular religious order: the Dominicans might have popularized the rosary, for instance, and that remained, but it is not annexed to them. As an example we might think of the scapular, a small piece of cloth worn next to the skin by lay people associated with various religious orders (as 'oblates' or 'tertiaries' who have taken their own sort of vows to live by the spirit of the order, but in the world).[19] The scapular serves as a physical reminder of their membership, as the habit does for those professed as monks, nuns or friars.

Down the centuries, Christians have found it helpful, often immensely helpful, to be associated with a particular order in this way, and in some traditions to be associated with a particular house of that order, from which they receive forms of devotion, a rule of life and partnership in the ongoing life of prayer. Such a lay person would be likely to make his or her retreats with that community and have a spiritual director from among their number. Such an oblate or tertiary is a real, not simply adjunct, member of the order. Someone who has taken vows of poverty, chastity and obedience will wear the habit of the order; a lay member might wear that piece of cloth, cut from the

---

19 'Tertiary' is derived from the Latin for 'third', where an order has first and second orders for men and women living in community, and a third for the sort of dispersed membership we are talking about.

same fabric as the habit, usually worn attached to a ribbon around the neck. Before the reforms it seemed sensible that the scapular of the Carmelites should be blessed by a Carmelite, the scapular of the Benedictines should be blessed by a Benedictine and so on, and indeed such blessings were 'reserved' to those orders. After the twentieth-century reforms centred around the Second Vatican Council, these strictures were considerably loosened, such that almost any priest or bishop can bless almost anything that can be blessed.[20]

This reservation of blessings might never have fitted particularly well within the disciplines of other churches. The Church of England, for instance, was never likely to police who blessed what. Today that sort of parity is found also in the Roman Catholic Church. All the same, both of those traditions, and others, might still maintain a sense that the category of 'most appropriate' is a narrower and richer one than the category of what is 'possible or legal'. Any priest might bless a scapular, but blessing operates by more than a simply utilitarian or minimalistic logic, and if the purpose of the scapular is as a tangible sign of one's bond to an order, it makes sense for it to be blessed by someone from that order.

In closing this section, it is worth noting that the one set of 'reserved' blessings that still holds quite forcefully are those associated with the bishop.[21] The correlation is not, certainly, as close as for some of the sacraments, where only a bishop can ordain in all of the ancient traditions. We might also think of the rule in the Anglican churches

---

20 'Reserved blessings shall be very few; reservations shall be in favour of bishops or ordinaries' (Constitution on the Sacred Liturgy – *Sacrosanctum Concilium*, §79).

21 See Constitution on the Sacred Liturgy – *Sacrosanctum Concilium*, §79.

that only a bishop can confirm (here reflecting the ancient Western practice). When it comes to blessings reserved to bishops, the judgement, again, is more a matter of what is appropriate than of what is strictly necessary. Some of it, even, is as obvious as asking what pattern it would be perverse for us not to adopt if we can. As an example, we can think of circumstances, perhaps in times of persecution, when a priest might bless a church building, but under any normal circumstance the episcopal churches see that as something for the bishop to do, as the chief pastor of the diocese, in whose name and by whose authority worship will be conducted there.

The other notable example is the blessing of the three oils used in the sacraments. Large quantities are typically blessed, by the bishop, at the Eucharist – the 'Chrism Mass' – that takes place during the day on Maundy Thursday (another Eucharist takes place in parish churches in the evening: 'the Mass of the Last Supper'). This is the principal service to express ministerial solidarity in the whole year. The clergy of the diocese, often joined by lay ministers, gather together with the bishop to reaffirm their ordination vows and celebrate the Eucharist on the day that it was given to the Church by Christ. The oils are blessed on this day so that they can be taken back to the parishes after the clergy have gathered with the bishop from all over the diocese.[22] In this way the blessing and distribution of the oils symbolize the connection of each church to the bishop, just as each of the sacraments in which they will be used is carried out in the authority conferred by the bishop.

---

22 The Church of England has a form of words that can be used, back in the parish, at the start of the Eucharist that evening, so that the oils can be received formally, with a public recognition of what has happened earlier.

That suggests a proper sense of interrelation in the fullest answer to our question, 'Who blesses?' The answer is 'The whole Church', and it is also (for most of the world's Christians) 'The bishop, and those to whom it has been delegated', meaning principally the priesthood. When any Christian blesses, in the realm that is proper to her, whether by word or deed, she acts in the name of the whole Church, and if the bishop is the principal minister of blessing in many churches, that is only because the bishop is thought to represent the whole Church and to be invested with authority to speak for the whole Church, at least in that locality.

Ultimately, beyond and in any of this, it is Christ who blesses in every blessing. In saying that, however, we should not undercut the sense in which Christ really does dignify us by giving us the task of blessing. He is not to us like a ventriloquist. We properly speak, and he speaks through us; we properly bless, and he blesses through us.

13

How Do We Bless?

The normal setting for a blessing will be a communal gathering of the church, met for worship, that is only a description of what is often most fitting. It does not suggest that every last blessing should be in a parish church on a Sunday morning; it does encourage us to bless in a public setting rather than in a private one, at least generally speaking, and to include a reading from the Bible, prayers of thanksgiving, and intercessions for the needs of the Church and the world. Sometimes blessings will take place in a church building; sometimes the setting may be a civic one, but even there or in a private home, we ought to think about how some, at least, of these other elements of liturgy can be brought in.

Where blessings take place in church, as many will (such as a service for commissioning a new ministry or a service to consecrate a new church), we might follow the example of the early Church in inserting a rite of blessing within a weekly or daily Eucharist. That would make particular sense when what we are blessing relates to the whole of the community, gathered together on that day, for instance with the blessing of a new church noticeboard or of vessels for Holy Communion. Where the blessing does not relate to the whole church community in quite that way, as for instance with the blessing of an icon to hang on a wall in someone's house, it may be more appropriate for the blessing to take place immediately after a service, whether that is a Eucharist or some other. That way worship is not 'clogged up' with ad hoc blessings, but a connection is still made with the worshipping life of the whole, since nothing about the Christian life is ever in fact entirely individual, to be negotiated outside the context of common membership of the Body of Christ.

When carried out in the context of communal worship like this, little more is likely to be needed than the prayer (or prayers) of blessing itself, perhaps combined with a related prayer of intercession. If the situation calls for slightly greater solemnity, a traditional verse and response can introduce the blessing: the priest says 'Our help is in the name of the Lord', to which the people reply 'Who hath made heaven and earth' (or the contemporary language equivalent).

Free-standing rites of blessing require a little more by way of deliberate structure. For instance, some sort of considered opening becomes more or less necessary to commence the rite. Commonly the greeting is 'In the name of the Father, and of the Son, and of the Holy Spirit', to which the congregation reply 'Amen'. This is followed by the verse and response just given. A short reading from the Bible is then to be encouraged. This sets what we are doing in the wider picture of God's relationship to his people and of the acts by which he has redeemed the world. This is another example of how a sharp distinction between blessing and salvation should not, and cannot, be maintained. Books of blessings will often include suggested short scriptural readings but the minister with a good knowledge of the Bible can be creative in finding a passage that strikes the right note. This reading may be followed by a short sermon or homily. If words of explanation are needed about what is going on, it may be advisable to incorporate them into the homily rather than interspersing comments, since that might work against the sense in which the elements speak for themselves. Before or after the prayer of blessing itself we can make intercessions connected to the situation or circumstance, and at the end a general blessing can be given upon all who have gathered. At one or more points a hymn, song or chant might be sung.

Complexity or Simplicity

As a general historical observation, prayers of blessing themselves became shorter in the twentieth century. Older sources often give them in several parts whereas modern equivalents often condense this to one reasonably short prayer. On the other hand, the rite itself, in which the blessing is embedded, tended to become longer, with the scriptural reading, the homily or address, the longer inter-cessory prayers and perhaps the inclusion of some songs. The reforms, in short, left us with simpler prayers of bless-ing but embedded within a longer whole.[1]

The argument against those older, multipartite prayers of blessing would be that elaborate forms may give the impression that the effect rests on the skill of the priest or bishop in doing just right something that is difficult to do. That would bring blessing very close to magic. On

---

1 For a summary of the older and newer typical structures of a rite of blessing, see Uwe Michael Lang, 'Theologies of Blessing: Origins and Characteristics of *De benedictionibus* (1984)', *Antiphon* 15.1 (2011), pp. 37–8. Even with the new sense in the Roman Catholic Church of a proper, multipartite structure for a blessing, there is dispensation for very short, single-prayer blessings in certain circumstances, for instance with the blessing of items of popular piety.

the other hand, a rite of blessing that is over before it has begun may be 'accessible' but can also be banal, and frequently is. Accessibility is often prized above all else in the contemporary Church, but we might question whether even those who are unfamiliar with the Church but come to it for blessing, dedication and consolation *really* want it to proceed with language that aspires to the semantic and lexicographical smoothness of an episode of a soap opera.

Moreover, a slightly more elaborate, multipartite blessing might suggest that the process of sanctification is not, characteristically, entirely straightforward. Blessing, after all, is a witness to the process of human sanctification, and as Evelyn Underhill put it:

> the work of sanctification as experienced by us in time is successive, as the consecrating action in the Eucharist is successive. God the Sanctifier is simultaneous and eternal; but man [and woman] the sanctified is ever subject to the law of growth and change.[2]

Material Elements and Gestures

Blessing is a physical business. We may sometimes bless intangible things, such as a Lenten intention, the formation of a new society or the arrival of the New Year, but even these are physically worked out: intentions are linked to actions, the society meets together and undertakes some definite work; time is woven together with space and, in that, forms the domain of physical existence as much as space does. And while we may sometimes bless intangible things, we much more often bless objects, places, persons –

---

2 Evelyn Underhill, *The Mystery of Sacrifice* (London: Longmans, Green & Co., 1938), p. 49.

all unmistakably physical. Even if, on All Souls' Day or some other occasion, we want to pronounce a blessing on the dead – those who have temporarily put off their physicality – we typically do so by blessing their grave.

If *what* is blessed is bound up with the physical, then so is the *way* we bless. Thomas Aquinas commented on this in a discussion of the outward aspects of predominantly sacramental worship. In God's gracious provision, he wrote, 'certain blessings using sensible things are provided for men and women, whereby one is washed, or anointed, or fed, or given drink, along with the expression of sensible words'. He went on to say that 'it is not astonishing if heretics who deny that God is the author of our body condemn such manifestations . . . They have not remembered that they are human beings.'[3] Christianity is full of blessings because it, like Judaism for instance, confesses God as creator and us as his creatures. Using water and gesture as part of the rite of blessing, for instance, serves to illustrate the way God draws all of creation into the work of redeeming and sanctifying the world.[4]

We have already discussed the most prominent gesture used in blessing, namely making the sign of the cross, and the most prominent material element, namely sprinkling with holy water. We mentioned them in Chapter 6 ('Blessing and Salvation in Ministry and Mission'), since they are two significant ways in which redemption is held before us in the practice of blessing: the reference of the sign is fairly obvious, while water recalls both the water of baptism – the first and primordial sacrament of salvation –

---

3 *Summa Contra Gentiles*, trans. Vernon J. Bourke (New York: Hanover House, 1955), III.119.3, 5.

4 I have written about this in Andrew Davison and Alison Milbank, *For the Parish: A Critique of Fresh Expressions* (London: SCM Press, 2010), pp. 28–40.

and all the associated imagery, such as the water of the Red See and the idea of an exodus from sin and death.

Practically speaking, the sign of the cross is typically made over the person, place or thing.[5] In the historical Western tradition the sign of the cross was always made in a blessing. Scholars have noted that this was no longer stipulated for Roman Catholics after the Second Vatican Council. This seems to be an omission, and in a 'clarification' of 2002 the Vatican's Congregation for Divine Worship and the Discipline of the Sacraments decreed that a blessing should always bear witness to Christ's passion by means of the sign of the cross, at least when the blessing is given by a bishop, priest or deacon.[6]

Holy water is typically sprinkled immediately after the blessing, either using some suitable leafy twig (rosemary being a common European equivalent to the hyssop plant used for the purpose of sprinkling in the Old Testament – only that was usually with *blood*) or a stick-like device, devised to retain water but imperfectly so, called an aspergillum. The water itself might be water that was blessed and retained after a baptism or water blessed for the purpose. The sacristy in a catholic-leaning parish will often contain a bottle of holy water. A prayer for the blessing of water can be found in most collections (although the priest might wish to analyse any given example to check whether it really blesses the water). It might be printed out and ingeniously glued to the outside of the bottle, so that it is always at hand when needed.

---

5 By tradition, a priest keeps the palm and the fingers of his or her hand flat, while a bishop raises his or her index and middle fingers, with the other two fingers and the thumb brought together in front of the palm.

6 Lang, 'Theologies of Blessing', p. 40.

As part of a blessing, sometimes in addition to sprinkling with holy water, what is to be blessed is also censed, which is to say that it is wafted with smoke from the burning of incense. As with the imagery of sprinkling with water (Numbers 8 and 19, picked up in Ezekiel 36.25), burning incense is also a biblical practice. As with water, the meanings and implications of incense are many: principally that it represents the prayers of the Church, ascending to God, and that it is associated with honouring dignified persons and therefore dignified things and places. The first set of associations come from the Scriptures and the second from the Greek and Roman world, where incense in a bowl on a chain (called a thurible) was carried before figures such as magistrates (originally, it would seem, to overcome the smell of the city and prevent it from offending them). Incense was also an expensive commodity, so the act of burning it to honour God, as we find in the Old Testament, carries obvious connotations of sacrifice. In each of these cases, with water and with incense, we can come up with a historical or analytic list of what they mean. Ultimately, however, the list will seem anaemic compared to their use in practice. The way to understand how these elements feature in the life of the Church is to experience them.

I have written before about the interrelation of references to the words and actions of the Church in worship.[7] That layering is so deep and so extensive that the only way to appreciate it to any degree is to live within it. Incense, again, provides a good example: it is – or can be – burnt at evening prayer, which picks up the offering of incense at the evening sacrifice in the Old Testament. It is used to honour holy things but also to prepare things for a holy

---

7 I wrote about this, and extended the analysis in a contrast with contemporary 'experimental liturgy', in *For the Parish*, pp. 108–13.

purpose. Those two uses blend into one another: we might put the emphasis on preparation when the bread, wine and worshippers are censed at the offertory in the Eucharist, before the consecration as the climax of the service, and we might put the emphasis on recognizing holiness when the sacred elements of the Eucharist are again censed, after the consecration. But that distinction only works so far: the things censed at the offertory are not treated as profane things to be purified but as God's holy creation – the people of God, bread, wine – who are now approaching their truest purpose in this holy act. Such an interweaving of meanings, we might also note, allows for one of the most extraordinary and moving associations in the entire liturgical life of the Church: the censing of the body at a funeral, as a holy thing.

If we cast our minds back to Chapter 7 we will also remember the suggestion that the urge to *place* things is not incidental to the business of blessing. For something to be blessed, as for it to be redeemed, is for it to be 'replaced', not in the sense of being substituted by something else but in the sense of coming to stand in a new place before God. That being so, we might be alert to the value of placing things to be blessed, or even, by a certain extension, the person to be blessed, whether that involves placing it in the sanctuary, laying it upon an altar or inviting the person or persons to stand before the altar.

Receiving a Blessing

No special posture or gesture is *needed* to receive a blessing but making the sign of the cross over oneself is traditional and widespread. Indeed, if someone is inclined only to make the sign infrequently it is most likely to be on reception of a blessing, and also possibly for the reception of absolution. That it is the paradigmatic Christian gesture needs little explanation. The history of how it came to be used as the sign of devout reception of something from God, whether blessing or forgiveness, is probably lost to us, but become that sign it has, for Christianity both East and West. It has become ubiquitous, just as blessings are ubiquitous in the life of the Church, or can be, which is the topic to which we turn in the next chapter through the cycle of the Christian year.

14

When Do We Bless?

This chapter will consider the prominent opportunities for blessings that arise over the course of the church year, as well as some of the traditional forms these blessings take. Before we move on to those, however, it is worth noting that in the common run of church services a blessing in the name of the Trinity is encountered by far the most often at the end of a service.[1] This blessing 'at the dismissal' deserves a few words. Its basic purpose is a form of commendation to God's care, which is an impulse that finds expression in ordinary human life and not simply the heightened circumstances of the liturgy, at least in many cultures. Even everyday phrases may involve an invocation of divine protection and blessing, or at least a remnant of it. The English word 'goodbye', after all, is a contraction of 'God be with ye'.

Liturgical blessings at the dismissal tend to have two parts. The first is variable and suits the season, the second is invariant and invokes the blessing of God, explicitly

---

1 Liturgical scholars are used, also, to seeing greeting as a form of blessing, both in a liturgy and more widely – as for instance Joseph Auneau in 'Blessing – A Biblical Theology', in Jean-Yves Lacoste (ed.), *Encyclopedia of Christian Theology* (London: Routledge, 2004), p. 218. I do not find the association particularly strong, not at least in the way greetings are given and received today.

named as Trinity.[2] For a blessing on a solemn occasion, the first part is often divided into three prayers, the congregation responding to each one with an 'Amen'. Today these are almost always addressed to successive Persons of the Trinity, although that was not always the rule in the Middle Ages. This threefold structure can be attributed either to the simple pleasingness of threefold repetition or to the template of the Aaronic blessing in Numbers 6.22–27, which also falls into three invocations.[3]

As an almost instinctive gesture, some Christians make the sign of the cross with holy water on both entering and leaving a church. Water for this purpose is kept in a bowl attached to the wall by the door, called a stoup. In this way we both prepare ourselves for the encounter with God in the church and for taking the gospel out into the world, using the sign of the cross and water that links us to our baptism.

Sunday

Blessing is closely associated with time. In the first chapter of Genesis, God blesses creatures (Gen. 1.22, 28) but he goes further when it comes to time, both 'blessing' the seventh day and 'hallowing' it (Gen. 2.3).[4] Time, like people, places and things, can be holy. In blessing it we both recognize its holiness and ourselves dedicate time. Against the backdrop

---

2 Richard Tatlock noted this pattern in both Galican and Anglo-Saxon sources in *An English Benedictional* (London: Faith Press, 1964), p. 11.

3 Tatlock, *An English Benedictional*, p. 12.

4 The point that the Sabbath receives this special attention comes in Jürgen Moltmann's *Source of Life*, p. 45, although his claim there, that the first thing that God sanctified or hallowed, in the biblical witness, was not a thing or a person or a place but a time, misses the blessing of sea creatures and human beings – but that may be a slip that occurs between the German and the English translation.

of our hectic manner of living it may be that blessing time – setting it aside, consecrating it from the ordinary cycle of everyday life and its demands – is among the most helpful and necessary forms of blessing. Following the example of Genesis 2, we can start with the Sabbath (Sunday for Christians), which is to be recognized as a holy day. The principle of one day in seven as rest is given to us in the Old Testament; Sunday, as that day, was established and made holy, in a shift with the New Covenant, by the resurrection of Christ. Blessing, as we have seen, involves an alignment with the world to come. We have this held before us, week by week, in the blessedness of Sunday, the eighth day, the first day of the new creation.[5] The rest of this section will cover suggestions for blessing over the course of the year. Prayers of blessing for almost all of these occasions can be found in Sean Finnegan's *Consecrations, Blessings and Prayers*.[6]

Advent and Christmastide

Progress through Advent can be marked, in church or at home, with the candles of an Advent wreath. *Consecrations, Blessings and Prayers* suggests using four white candles.[7] At least in the Church of England, candles in the liturgical colours are more commonly used: either four purple candles for the Sundays of Advent and a white candle in the

---

5 Relatively little has been written about the significance of *Sunday*. From a previous century we have W. B. Trevelyan's *Sunday* in the Oxford Library of Practical Theology (London: Longmans, Green & Co., 1902). In Portuguese and Italian, for those who can read those languages, there is *Domingo: Nascimento de Uma Nova Criação/La Domenica* by João Guedes (Sān Paulo: Ave Maria, 2007; Rome: Città Nova, 2009).

6 Sean Finnegan (ed.), *Consecrations, Blessings and Prayers* (London: Canterbury Press, 2005).

7 Finnegan, *Consecrations, Blessings and Prayers*, p. 201.

centre to light at Christmas, or three purple candles and one in pink or rose (the third candle), since the Third Sunday of Advent ('Gaudete' Sunday) is observed in that colour in more catholic-minded parishes. Wreaths may also be displayed on house doors, and these too can be blessed.

The suggestions for Christmas should be relatively obvious, starting with the nativity set or crib. Objects such as these call for two sorts of blessing. When it is first bought and put to use, we can dedicate it to the purpose that it will fulfil year after year. Then, each Christmas, we bless it for that season's display. In the first case we dedicate the *objects*; in the second case we bless that particular *act* of laying out as a witness to the incarnation.[8] The same twofold pattern might apply to any durable item dedicated to use in worship but only brought out each year for a specific period, such as the permanent elements of an Easter garden.

Moving on, we come to the New Year. The Church has not always known quite what to do with this observance, perhaps because it has its own cycle, which begins with Advent Sunday, and perhaps because there has seemed something rather irreligious about popular celebrations of New Year as they currently stand. These are not necessarily hostile to religion, it is just that they are rather unusual in the progression of the year in floating largely free of any involvement of the Church in the deep-seated cultural imagination. At least that is the perspective from England. In other countries, New Year may be a more obviously, and easily, Christian celebration.

---

8 Finnegan, *Consecrations, Blessings and Prayers*, gives two rites, one for use at home (p. 205) and the other for use in church at the Midnight Mass (pp. 204–5). Some parish priests like to bless the nativity set again at the main, perhaps family-orientated, Christmas-morning service. For the sake of theological tidiness, it might be better to adapt the prayers so as not actually to be *blessing* it for a second time in a day.

If we were to think of ways to mark the turn of the year with prayer, some 'blessing of the New Year' might be possible as a collective act. On an individual level, a pastor might want to offer a listening ear as to people's choice of New Year's resolutions, with advice if it is wanted, and a blessing.

Anciently, Epiphany was a time for gifts. Some traditions ask for contributions towards the supplies needed to run the church over the year ahead. The link here is probably through donations of incense (or donations towards incense), picking up on one of the Magi's gifts, and by extension, of donations towards altar bread and wine, candles and so on.

Epiphany is also a time for blessing homes, probably because the Magi are described as 'entering the house' (Matt. 2.11) in which Jesus and his parents were to be found. The Latin prayer that can be used on this occasion, *Christus mansionem benedicat* – meaning '[May], Christ bless this house' – is a sort of acrostic pun on the first letters of the traditional names of the wise men: Caspar, Melchior and Balthasar. As the blessing is made, these letters can be inscribed on the lintel of the door with chalk, along with a reference to the year. So, for instance, in 2015 the lettering might look like this, with the sign of the cross interspersed: 20 + C + M + B + 15. How this blessing is given might differ from situation to situation. In some places the priest travels round the parish, visiting the homes of those who have asked for the blessing. Alternatively, sticks of chalk may be blessed at the Epiphany Eucharist and members of the congregation sent on their way with a piece – and perhaps a piece of paper printed with the prayer and a diagram of what is traditionally inscribed – for them to perform the act themselves when they get home. In Continental Europe the chalk is sometimes given to gangs of children, who go off to perform the blessing. A house might also be blessed at any stage during the year, for instance when new occupants have moved in.

In rural communities, Plough Sunday may be observed on the Sunday after the Epiphany. It provides an opportunity to ask for God's blessing on crops and the earth by blessing farm instruments (classically the plough), which were brought into church, or by blessing seed, or both.[9]

The next major feast of the Church is the Presentation of Christ in the Temple (2 February), which is traditionally called Candlemas because of the association of this feast with light. On this occasion the priest Simeon acclaimed the infant Christ as 'A light to lighten the Gentiles, and the glory of thy people Israel' (Luke 2.32, AV). This is the point of the year when candles were traditionally blessed – for use in church over the year ahead but also to be distributed to the faithful to take home.

Candlemas is a naturally winning celebration, rarely received with anything but affection and joy by all who encounter it. Within contemporary liturgical practice it has received prominence as the feast that brings Christmastide – the 40 days of Christmas – to an end, and as a pivot when our thoughts begin to turn from Christmas towards Lent, Holy Week and Easter.

The day after Candlemas is the feast of St Blaise, Martyr and Bishop of Sebastea in present-day Turkey, who died around the year 316. He is the patron saint of people suffering from diseases of the throat, and so a tradition has grown up for blessing throats on his day. The association comes from the story that he healed a boy who was choking to death on

---

9 The Church of England provides liturgical material for Plough Sunday in *Common Worship: Times and Seasons* (London: Church House Publishing, 2006), pp. 607–8, although the blessings themselves, of the plough and of the seed, show a disappointing discomfort with actually blessing physical things. As with other such half-hearted prayers, they could be modified so as to bestow a blessing with more forthright confidence. The supporting liturgical material is strong.

a fish bone. This blessing is usually performed with two large candles, conveniently blessed the day before, bound together with a red ribbon (red, since Blaise was a martyr). Practically speaking it is wise to tie the ribbon rather loosely so that the candles form an X-shape, the top end of which can be pressed gently against the throat of anyone who wishes to receive the blessing. This works most easily if the ribbon is tied closer to the bottom of the candles rather than in the middle.[10]

Lent, Holy Week and Easter

Ash Wednesday follows, marking the beginning of Lent. On this day of penitence the custom is to receive the sign of the cross, in ash, on one's forehead. The ash can conveniently be made by burning palm crosses given out the year before. Students of chemistry will confirm that the ash is likely to be blacker if the palms are burnt in a slightly enclosed container. The ash is blessed as part of the rite and typically includes a prayer that it will help us to remember our mortality and turn our minds to penitence. Any such blessing can be accompanied by sprinkling with holy water. On this occasion there is all the more to be said for this – which may in any case be standard practice for almost any blessings – since moistening the ash towards a paste allows it to transfer more easily onto the skin. The water should suffice to make the right consistency, although a drop of olive oil or glycerine would go even further for those enterprising clergy looking for the perfect mess with which to ash.

Recalling our thoughts about New Year's resolutions, Lenten intentions are just as much worthy of receiving a blessing, perhaps even more so. Opportunity might be

---

10 A suitable prayer is found in Finnegan, *Consecrations, Blessings and Prayers*, pp. 215–16.

found on Ash Wednesday for people to express their hopes and commitments for the season, and to receive a blessing individually. This sort of encouragement to approach Lent seriously might even come usefully before Ash Wednesday, perhaps as an exhortation on the Sunday before Lent, with space put aside for people to come for a blessing after any of the services on that day.

We have already mentioned palm crosses, which are blessed and distributed on Palm Sunday, the Sunday before Easter, and in Chapter 12 we discussed the blessing of oils on Maundy Thursday. The next major blessing is perhaps the most highly charged blessing of the entire year: the blessing of the paschal candle, which traditionally takes place during the Easter Vigil, either late on Saturday night or early on Sunday morning. Easter is the 'feast of feasts' and few who are in the habit of going to an Easter Vigil would deny that this is the 'service of services'.

The blessing of the candle takes place at the beginning of the service as the clergy and congregation gather round the newly kindled fire. The Vigil is a solemn and joyful occasion – two adjectives often falsely supposed to be in opposition – and this opening blessing of the paschal candle is itself a moment of both. Most traditions follow the same pattern. The candle is blessed with both words and gestures, the priest tracing out the shapes of the various symbols: a cross, an alpha and omega, the numerals of the current year. These are typically already drawn or printed onto the candle by the manufacturers in advance. In the contemporary rite of the Church of England, as an example, these are the words and rubrics:

As the vertical of the cross is traced the president says
    Christ, yesterday and today,
As the horizontal is traced the president says
    the beginning and the end,

As the Alpha is traced
   Alpha
As the Omega is traced
   and Omega,
As the first number of the year is traced the president says
   all time belongs to him,
As the second number is traced
   and all ages;
As the third number is traced
   to him be glory and power,
As the fourth number is traced
   through every age and for ever.
   Amen.[11]

Five incense grains are then stuck into the candle to represent Christ's wounds (two in his hands or wrists, two in his feet or ankles and one in his side). These grains are often incorporated into pins made for the purpose, to make the insertion easier. During this action a prayer is made:

By his holy and glorious wounds
may Christ our Lord guard and keep us.
Amen.

Finally, the candle is lit from the new fire, representing the resurrection, with another prayer:

May the light of Christ, rising in glory,
banish all darkness from our hearts and minds.

---

11 *Common Worship: Times and Seasons*, p. 409.

A little later in the service the blessing of the candle is taken further, with the ancient hymn known as the *Exsultet* or, in Latin, *Praeconium Paschale*, meaning Easter praises or Easter proclamation. It is traditionally sung by a deacon. The precise origin of the text is unknown but it, or its precursors, go back to the times of the Fathers. As such it is one of the most authoritative texts outside of Scripture, having been taken to the Church's heart for the considerable part of its life. The text praises Christ, situating the victory of the resurrection within the widest story of redemption. It can, however, also be seen as part of the 'blessing' of the candle, in that the candle itself, representing Christ the risen daystar, features prominently.

The Easter morning Eucharist often has a 'family' focus to it, and one way to foster this is to have an Easter-egg hunt. *Consecrations, Blessings and Prayers* provides a prayer for the blessing of eggs, which symbolize both new life and the emptiness of the tomb after the resurrection. Some churches hold an Easter lunch, typically of lamb, or an Easter breakfast after the Vigil. The blessing of a feast on this occasion is one of the most ancient practices of blessing to have survived from the early Church.[12]

The Sunday before the Ascension is Rogation Sunday, the time for processions to pronounce a blessing the fields, which we have already discussed (see pp. 130–2). A litany is often recited; examples would include the litany in the Book of Common Prayer or a litany of the saints.[13]

---

12 See Finnegan, *Consecrations, Blessings and Prayers*, p. 227, for a suitable form of words.

13 See Finnegan, *Consecrations, Blessings and Prayers*, pp. 230–5, for the latter. The Church of England's *Common Worship: Times and Seasons* provides good Rogation petitions to insert into a standard litany, in both traditional and contemporary language.

For Christians with a sense of the poetic gesture, the Feast of the Ascension has often suggested climbing something high. As an undergraduate I was proud to have had a hand in instituting a still-thriving tradition of climbing the college tower on Ascension morning, for a brief service of readings, hymns and prayers. The chaplain found it perfectly natural, from that vantage point, to pronounce a blessing upon the college and locality, laid out as a vista before us.

After the Ascension comes Pentecost, which has rather little by way of 'physical culture', at least in my British experience. Traditions from other countries might provide suggestions for observing the descent of the Holy Spirit, with blessings attached, for instance with food – often a cake – associated with this feast.

Trinity Sunday and Beyond

Trinity Sunday does not particularly suggest practices associated with blessing, for all Christians find something archetypal in giving blessings in the name of God as Three-in-One. The Thursday after, however, is the Feast of Corpus Christi, which is very much a time for blessing. Some churches finish the service with a rite known simply as Benediction, when the congregation is blessed with the consecrated host or communion bread. The particularity of what is going on here – that the blessing is given with 'something' (here the blessed sacrament) – is not entirely unique, although this is the only case that most Christians are likely to encounter any more. The other example might be blessing with the relic of a saint, perhaps on that saint's feast day.

Between the Eucharist itself and this solemn blessing it is not uncommon for a procession to be interleaved, where the church community takes that which is so precious to them – the presence of Christ in the sacramental elements – out into the world, bearing witness to all of this in the streets. (A procession such as this can take place on other occasions, such as the Patronal Feast.) This is a joyful affair, with the amassed spectacle of the best vestments, much singing, trumpets if one can find players, children scattering rose petals, all the usual elements of a procession – smoke, lights and the processional cross – and some unusual ones, such as a canopy over the blessed sacrament and banners. A procession of this sort might be considered to be a blessing of its own – the hallowing of the neighbourhood with the presence of Christ – but that should not stop us from giving a particular blessing on the way, if that is appropriate. In the parish where I served my curacy, the procession went through the green at the very centre of the estate, and that was a good place to stop to bless the whole community from that central location.

Ordinations happen at various times throughout the year, and the seasons will vary from tradition to tradition. In my own church, the Church of England, the two principal seasons are the end of June (Petertide, associated with the feast on the 29 June, which is variously given to St Peter or to both St Peter and St Paul) and the end of September (Michaelmas, the Feast of St Michael and All Angels on 29 September). I will place this section on ordination here, linking it to the end of June. A priestly ordination is followed soon after by a priest's first celebration of the Eucharist. This is traditionally a time for blessing – the first time that the priest blesses people in that new capacity. The practice of 'first blessings' is conveniently placed after the end of the first Eucharist, perhaps in a side chapel. The queue can be rather long. Those who were not able to attend the first Eucharist might wish to ask the priest for a 'first blessing' on the next occasion when they meet.

The medieval occasion for giving thanks for crops in England was Lammas (meaning 'Loaf-Mass', from the

Anglo-Saxon *Hlafmaesse*). It was held on the first of August, when a loaf, newly baked from the new grain, was offered to God within a Mass. This observance was abolished at the Reformation but the day itself – Lammas and Lammastide – was preserved in the calendar of the Book of Common Prayer and in some local customs and place names, for instance in public fields called Lammas Land (as, for instance, in Cambridge and London), which were open to public grazing after the harvest; that is, from Lammas Day until the Feast of the Annunciation (25 March).

A parish might choose to give thanks to God for the provision of the earth in this way, either on 1 August or at some other time, ideally baking a loaf themselves from the new grain, grown as locally as possible. This loaf might be used to provide the bread for the Eucharist, and portions of any unconsecrated bread might be given out at the end of the service. The Church of England's *Common Worship: Times and Seasons* provides liturgical material for this service, including a prayer for the offering of the bread and the following paragraph of introduction:

Brothers and sisters in Christ, the people of God in ancient times presented to the Lord an offering of first-fruits as a sign of their dependence upon God for their daily bread. At this Lammastide, we bring a newly baked loaf as our offering in thanksgiving to God for his faithfulness.

Jesus said, 'I am the bread of life; those who come to me shall never be hungry and those who believe in me shall never thirst.'

The Lammas tradition, or the religious urge associated with it to thank God for the harvest, came back into widespread use in England in the nineteenth century, although with the presentation of crops – often in the form of a display – rather than with the Lammas Loaf. This revival of harvest thanksgiving was officially recognized by the Church of England in 1862, and is often celebrated in October, when the harvest is complete.

Parishes with church schools, or priests with good relationships with a local school, may want to consider the place of blessing in the lives of those institutions. One priest from a college where I taught found enthusiastic take-up for the offer to bless school bags and satchels to mark the beginning of the academic year.

Perhaps the final opportunity for blessing, before the year begins again with Advent Sunday, is the All Souls-tide blessing of graves. When a church has its own graveyard this blessing, in the form of a procession, can take place immediately after the All Souls' Eucharist. The final blessing and dismissal might be deferred until the end of the procession, in order to make it an integral part of the service itself. During the service a litany or various psalms might be recited. The Roman Catholic Church's *Book of Blessings*, which was discussed in Chapter 9, suggests Psalms 25, 27, 42, 116, 118, 130 and 143 or portions of them.[14] *Consecrations, Blessings and Prayers* provides a particularly well-thought-out service.[15] Since the All Souls' service is highly charged enough already, and the best way to follow it would be with a cup of tea or glass of wine and opportunity for friendly, pastoral conversations, the All Souls-tide blessing of graves might sensibly be deferred until the Sunday after.

---

14 Characteristically, it offers almost nothing by way of blessing of the graves, but only the assembled congregation and any newly erected headstones.

15 Finnegan, *Consecrations, Blessings and Prayers*, pp. 238–41.

Conclusion

In the West the Christian faith is now known profoundly poorly. Against that background, blessings present an opportunity for Christians to bear witness to God and indeed to surprisingly many interrelated aspects of Christian belief. Blessings take in the whole of human life and experience and relate it to God – from the blessing of a pregnant mother to the blessing of a grave.

In this the witness of blessings is realistic about evil and fallenness. That is useful, since those around us retain an awareness of evil, even in the profoundly un-metaphysical twenty-first century: awareness of evil could hardly fail to remain in the twenty-first century, given the blood-soaked state in which humanity left the twentieth. Indeed, we find evil often perversely celebrated in films and novels. If offers of blessings are taken up (and if they are offered they will be taken up), then awareness that all is not right with the world will be an important reason.

At its heart, however, blessing is not simply about evil or protection. It is celebratory and grateful for the world that God has given us – it is about life. That is no bad thing to stress, given that when Christianity does draw comment today, it is often presented as mean-spirited and world-denying. By a tragic reversal, this most incarnational of faiths is seen as dualistic, and rejected as such. Bringing the ministry of blessing to greater prominence might do much to correct that reputation for mean-spiritedness, which so little characterized authentic Christianity.

Our culture is much at ease with communication by non-verbal means while, by contrast, the prospect of opening the discussion of theological topics in an abstract way is less promising than ever. With that in mind we can remember that blessing is usually helpfully visual and kinetic. Indeed, it can be positively theatrical, Rogationtide or Corpus Christi processions providing obvious examples. We hear calls today to be creative in our mission. Blessings offer boundless possibilities in mission and ministry since the bounds of blessing are only the limits of that which is and can be good. There is enormous flexibility here, and room for creativity, allowing us to meet whatever the circumstances may be with a 'good word' about God and about creation.[1]

The tradition of blessings has much to teach us of ethical significance, not least in terms of a respectful and grateful attitude towards creation. The association of blessing with life and abundance should act as a spur for addressing deprivation, and yet the startling teaching in the Bible as to where true blessedness is to be found also stands as a marked challenge to a culture of greed and excess.

Perhaps most important of all is the thought that a revival of the practice of blessing can be a part of a deepening Christian discipleship. Two features are entwined here: blessings foster a deepening awareness of God, his world, ourselves and what matters most; and alongside that, and in each case, they also provide a way to respond: in concert

---

1 The *Catechism of the Catholic Church* (London: Burns & Oates, 2004; see also www.vatican.va/archive/ENG0015/_INDEX.HTM), §1668, makes this point about the 'sacramentals' in general, of which blessings form a pivotal part.

with the natural order although also pointing beyond it, in ministry and in mission, in acknowledging the world's fallenness and bearing a part in putting it right, in relation to Christ, in consecration, in working out our vocation, in praise, in recognition and in thanksgiving.

Bibliography

Some churches have their own official collections of blessings, as with the Roman Catholic Church's *Book of Blessings* and the older *Rituale Romanum* or Roman Ritual. The weaknesses of the former collection have been discussed above. For a happy medium between banality and obscurity, I recommend Sean Finnegan's collection, *Consecrations, Blessings and Prayers*.

Books of Blessings

Church of England, *Common Worship: Times and Seasons* (London: Church House Publishing, 2013).

Finnegan, Sean (ed.), *Consecrations, Blessings and Prayers* (London: Canterbury Press, 2005). See recommendation above.

International Commission on English in the Liturgy of the Roman Catholic Church, *Book of Blessings* (Collegeville, MN: Liturgical Press, 1989). The US edition is authorized by other Roman Catholic bishops' conferences, for instance the Catholic Bishops' Conference of England and Wales.

Magee, Brian, *The Veritas Book of Blessing Prayers* (Dublin: Veritas, 1989). In the spirit of the Second Vatican Council, the prayers are direct and contemporary but serious and with a strong pastoral orientation. Notes are provided about what might need to be prepared in advance, and there is advice on some of the more highly charged situations that the book addresses.

Underhill, Evelyn, *Eucharistic Prayers from the Ancient Liturgies* (London: Longmans, Green & Co., 1939). Contains examples of consecratory prayers from the eucharistic rites, especially of the Eastern and Oriental Churches.

Weller, Philip T., *The Roman Ritual: In Latin and English with Rubrics and Plainchant Notation* (Boonville, NY: Preserving Christian Publications, 2007). A translation of the older *Rituale Romanum*.

Secondary Literature on Blessing

Auneau, Joseph and Pierre-Marie Gy, 'Blessing', in Jean-Yves Lacoste (ed.), *Encyclopedia of Christian Theology* (London: Routledge, 2004), pp. 218–20.

Ball, Ann A., *Handbook of Catholic Sacramentals* (Huntington, IN: Our Sunday Visitor, 1991).

Bowler, Kate, *Blessing: A History of the American Prosperity Gospel* (New York: Oxford University Press, 2013).

Chupungco, Anscar J., *Sacraments and Sacramentals* (Collegeville, MN: Liturgical Press, 2000).

Collins, Mary, David Noel Power and Marcus Lefébure, *Blessing and Power* (Edinburgh: T. & T. Clark, 1985).

Coupland, Simon, *Success: A Biblical Exploration* (Cambridge: Grove Books, 2002).

Donovan, Marcus, *Sacramentals* (London: Society of SS Peter & Paul, 1925).

Grüneberg, Keith, *Blessing: Biblical Meaning and Pastoral Practice* (Cambridge: Grove Books, 2003).

Harbin, Michael A., *The Promise and the Blessing: A Historical Survey of the Old and New Testaments* (Grand Rapids, MI: Zondervan, 2005).

Jounel, P., 'Blessings', in Aimé-Georges Martimort, Robert Cabié et al., *The Church at Prayer: Volume III – The Sacraments* (Collegeville, MN: Liturgical Press, 1988), pp. 263–84.

Lancaster, Sarah Heaner, *The Pursuit of Happiness: Blessing and Fulfillment in Christian Faith* (Eugene, OR: Wipf & Stock, 2011).

Lang, Uwe Michael, 'Theologies of Blessing: Origins and Characteristics of *De benedictionibus* (1984)', *Antiphon* 15.1 (2011), pp. 27–46.

Lathrop, Gordon, *Holy Ground: A Liturgical Cosmology* (Minneapolis, MN: Fortress Press, 2003).

Lenning, Larry G., *Blessing in Mosque and Mission* (Pasadena, CA: William Carey Library, 1980).

Lovasik, Lawrence G., *The Sacramentals of the Church* (New York: Catholic Book Publishing Company, 1986). A booklet for children. The text is good but the illustrations might not be thought so helpful today – all very 1950s, rosy-cheeked and Anglo-Saxon.

Macquarrie, John, 'Benediction of the Blessed Sacrament', in *Paths in Spirituality* (London: SCM Press, 1972), pp. 94–102.

Parker, Russ, *Rediscovering the Ministry of Blessing* (London: SPCK, 2014).

Rivard, Derek A., *Blessing the World: Ritual and Lay Piety in Medieval Religion* (Washington, DC: Catholic University of America Press, 2009).

Stevenson, Kenneth, *Nuptial Blessing: A Study of Christian Marriage Rites* (London: Alcuin Club, 1982). This survey is exhaustive, up to the time of writing. The remit is much wider than the blessings mentioned in the title, although blessings in the marriage service are discussed thoroughly.

Underhill, Evelyn, *The Mystery of Sacrifice: A Meditation on the Liturgy* (London: Longmans, Green & Co., 1938). For the section on consecration in particular.

Westermann, Claus, *Blessing in the Bible and the Life of the Church* (Philadelphia, PA: Fortress Press, 1978).

Biblical Index

Index of People

Subject Index

absolution 70–1, 173, 186

abundance 15–19, 27, 29, 30–47, 50, 66, 75, 163–5, 170–1, 201–2, *see also* progeny, prosperity, rogation

Advent 189–90

All Souls' Day 182, 200, *see also* graveyard

altar, 14, 107, 111, 124, 126, 144–5, 157, 184, 190

anamnesis 20–1, 91, *see also* blessing as recognition

anathema 56–7, 110

angels 13, 16–17, 22, 45, 158

anniversary 120, 154

Annunciation to the Blessed Virgin 42, 94

anointing 93, 126–7, 130–2, 140–1, 154, 182

Apostolic Tradition 6–7, 140

Ascension of Jesus 3, 146, 150, 196–7

Ash Wednesday 141, 173, 193–4

atonement, theories of 62–4, 66–7

baptism 27–8, 51, 69, 71–2, 93, 96, 102, 104, 124, 126, 132, 141, 146, 152–4, 162, 167, 182–3, 188

of Christ 51

barak 5, 45, 54

beatification 45

beatus/beata, as happy 45–6

benedictus, as blessed 45

bishops 15, 103, 109, 124–6, 130, 167, 175–7, 183

blessed, who is considered 39–47

blessing

Aaronic 188

and action, 118–21, 169–70, *see also* blessing and vocation, intentionality

and Bible reading 178–9

and intercession 178, 180, *see also* blessing and beseeching

and communality 43–4, 85

and protection 73–4

and responsibility 14–15, 22

and natural order 113–8

as beseeching 19–22, 91, 105–6, 125–7, 150–2, 162, 169, 187

as habit 8, 21

as impartation of vocation 13–14

as praise 3, 5–6, 9–11, 12, 21, 48, 64, 100–1, 119, 138, 143, 150, 152, 160, 169, 196, 203, *see also* blessing God

as protection 73, 93–4, 104, 140–2, 187, 201, *see also* evil

as recognition 6–11, 12, 20–1, 84–6, 100, 118–21, 161–2

as redirection 14–15, 109–11, 118–21

as sanctification, *see* consecration

213

SUBJECT INDEX